A. Cleveland

Christian Ballads

A. Cleveland

Christian Ballads

ISBN/EAN: 9783743305137

Manufactured in Europe, USA, Canada, Australia, Japa

Cover: Foto ©Lupo / pixelio.de

Manufactured and distributed by brebook publishing software (www.brebook.com)

A. Cleveland

Christian Ballads

CHRISTIAN BALLADS.

BY
ARTHUR CLEVELAND COXE.

REVISED EDITION.

He appointed singers before the LORD, that should praise the BEAUTY OF HOLINESS.—*Chronicles.*

NEW YORK:
D. APPLETON AND COMPANY.
443 & 445 BROADWAY.
1864.

ENTERED, according to Act of Congress, in the year 1864, by

A. CLEVELAND COXE,

In the Clerk's Office of the District Court for the Southern District of New York

TO

JOHN HENRY HOBART.

My Dear Hobart,

I dedicate these Ballads to you, as a duty and as a pleasure: as a duty, because but for you they would never have been written; and as a pleasure, because I rejoice to associate my name with yours, in any thing, however humble, which I am permitted to do for the Church of God. I need not say, that I consider it in happy harmony with their design, that I am privileged to inscribe them to the inheritor of a name whose praise is in all the Churches.

I know that to you at least they will not be unacceptable. The glistening dews of a Christian boyhood are fast drying up from both of us; but here are some results of rambling talks, and rural walks, and holiday diversions, which for years we have enjoyed together, and which through life will be dear to memory, as having gradually led us to find our best delight, and to choose our portion, in the amiable dwellings of the Lord of Hosts.

Yours, my dear Hobart,
A. C. C.

Chelsea, New York,
June 28, 1840.

PREFACE

TO THE ILLUSTRATED EDITION.

A PROPOSAL of the Messrs. APPLETON, to publish an illustrated edition of the Christian Ballads, recalled to the author's attention a little work which graver occupations had almost dismissed from his thoughts. He was startled to discover that five-and-twenty years have passed since they first appeared.

While giving them the benefit of such a revision as might not materially change the form in which the public has been pleased to accept them, he was led to some reflections, which he ventures to think may be properly presented as a preface to this edition, commemorative as it is of a quarter-century in the history of the book.

Of its faults nobody can be so sensible as the author himself. The Ballads were produced and published for ephemeral circulation, and with no anticipation of the favour with which they have been constantly demanded, in successive editions, in Europe and America. They were the outpourings of the honest convictions of the writer's heart, and he aimed only to wake up the consciousness of his countrymen to the value of many things which they seemed to underestimate. They were not designed as religious poems in the popular sense, but they were intended to show that there are natural relations between genuine religion and good taste.

Failing to observe this drift and purpose of the Ballads, they were censured, on their first appearance, as if they had aimed to supplant the substance of religion, by its merest accidents. They were compared with rude but hearty lyrics of uneducated piety, and described as wholly inferior to them, in all that moves the soul to penitence and prayer. Nothing can be more true; but nothing could be more unjust than the comparison. Hymns are one thing, and ballads are quite another; and he who wrote these Ballads would be the first to maintain that the writer of a single hymn, that is worthy of its name, has produced something more precious than all the verses that he ever penned.

On revising them he is further impressed with a conviction that their merit, whatever it may be, is comparatively much less, at the present time, than when they were produced, their currency having diminished their intrinsic worth. Thus, they abound in forms of expression which were fresh and original when they appeared, but which have since become tediously familiar in this kind of verse. One word which he timidly coined, to express the perspective lines of moonlight on the waters, has passed into common use; and architectural terms which once were rare and poetical, have become so ordinary and mechanical as to deprive some verses, in which they are employed, of all claims to even the low merit of freedom from prosaic diction.

It is gratifying to observe the progress of our civilization and the improvement of the popular taste in art; but the author must beg his readers to remember that many things which are now familiar to everybody in America, were wholly unknown among us when these Ballads were produced. Their author was obliged to imagine much that may now be seen in almost every part of the land. When he wrote them, there was not a church in the country which could sustain any other than the most moderate pretensions to architectural correctness in design or decoration. He had never seen more than a few panes of stained glass in a church window, nor heard a complete chime of bells; and there was not to be seen, on this Continent, so far as he is informed, an open roof, or a well-defined chancel, or genuine aisles, or a nave with a clere-story. Floral decorations were almost unknown, and children were not provided with a single carol. It has often been asserted, by generous critics, like the late Dr. Croswell, that the publication of the Ballads contributed largely to introduce the change in popular taste; but the author is well aware that his own delight in such things was the product, in a great measure, of what Dr. Croswell and Bishops Doane and Hopkins, and Dr. Muhlenberg, with others that might be named, had been doing before. From the progressive future he anticipates a great reduction in the popularity of his verses. They will fail to please when what is now agreeable in fancy becomes common in fact; and it is the height of his ambition with regard to them, that they may yet do something to hasten the time when they will be quite superfluous.

has been so little encouraged by subsequent events, may yet be drawn forth afresh by such a change of policy in England, as may secure to her the natural alliance which, but a little while ago, she might have made her own forever, and with which she might confront the world, and go forth anew to the noblest enterprises for the welfare of mankind.

A. C. C.

Rectory, Calvary Church,
 Gramercy Square, N. Y., *Sept.* 1864.

CONTENTS.

Hymn of Boyhood,	11
St. Sacrament,	17
Antioch,	33
Dreamland,	39
Carol,	47
Lament,	54
Ember-Prayers,	57
England,	61
Chronicles,	72
The Chimes of England,	84
Scotland,	88
Seabury's Mitre,	95
Rustic Churches,	98
Churchyards,	102
Trinity, Old Church,	108
Trinity, New Church,	113
The Spire-Cross,	118
Oratories,	123
Wayside Homes,	126
Little Woodmere,	128
Desolations,	136

Chelsea,	139
Vigils,	144
Matin Bells,	149
The Curfew,	152
Wildminster,	156
Nashotah,	160
St. Silvan's Bell,	166
Daily Service,	172
Christmas Carol,	176
Christening,	180
The Calendar,	184
The Soul-Dirge,	188
The Church's Daughter,	192
I love the Church,	198
Italian Versions,	205
Notes,	223

CHRISTIAN BALLADS.

Hymn of Boyhood.

One thing have I desired of the LORD, which I will require, even that I may dwell in the house of the LORD all the days of my life, to behold the fair beauty of the LORD, and to visit His temple.—*Psalter.*

I.

FIRST dear thing that ever I loved
Was a mother's gentle eye,
That smiled, as I woke on the dreamy couch
That cradled my infancy.
I never forget the joyous thrill
That smile in my spirit stirred,

Nor how it could charm me against my will,—
Till I laughed like a joyous bird.

II.

And the next fair thing that ever I loved
  Was a bunch of summer flowers,
With odours, and hues, and loveliness,
  Fresh as from Eden's bowers.
I never can find such hues agen,
  Nor smell such a sweet perfume ;
And if there be odours as sweet as then,
  'Tis I that have lost the bloom.

III.

And the next dear thing that ever I loved
  Was a fawn-like little maid,
Half-pleased, half-awed by the frolic boy
  That tortured her doll, and played :
I never can see the gossamere
  Which rude rough zephyrs tease,
But I think how I tossed her flossy locks
  With my whirling bonnet's breeze.

IV.

And the next good thing that ever I loved
  Was a bow-kite in the sky ;

And a little boat on the brooklet's surf,
    And a dog for my company:
And a jingling hoop, with many a bound
    To my measured strike and true;
And a rocket sent up to the firmament,
    When Even was out so blue.

V.

And the next fair thing I was fond to love
    Was a field of wavy grain,
Where the reapers mowed; or a ship in sail
    On the billowy, billowy main:
And the next was a fiery prancing horse
    That I felt like a man to stride;
And the next was a beautiful sailing boat
    With a helm it was hard to guide.

VI.

And the next dear thing I was fond to love
    Is tenderer far to tell;
'Twas a voice, and a hand, and a gentle eye
    That dazzled me with its spell:
And the loveliest things I had loved before
    Were only the landscape now,
On the canvass bright where I pictured her,
    In the glow of my early vow.

VII.

And the next good thing I was fain to love
  Was to sit in my cell alone,
Musing o'er all these lovely things,
  Forever, forever flown.
Then out I walked in the forest free,
  Where wantoned the autumn wind,
And the coloured boughs swung shiveringly,
  In harmony with my mind.

VIII.

And a spirit was on me that next I loved,
  That ruleth my spirit still,
And maketh me murmur these sing-song words,
  Albeit against my will.
And I walked the woods till the winter came,
  And then did I love the snow;
And I heard the gales, through the wildwood aisles,
  Like the LORD's own organ blow.

IX.

And the bush I had loved in my greenwood walk,
  I saw it afar away,
Surpliced with snows, like the bending priest
  That kneels in the church to pray:

And I thought of the vaulted fane, and high,
  Where I stood when a little child,
Awed by the lauds sung thrillingly,
  And the anthems undefiled.

X.

And again to the vaulted church I went,
  And I heard the same sweet prayers,
And the same full organ-peals upsent,
  And the same soft soothing airs;
And I felt in my spirit so drear and strange,
  To think of the race I ran,
That I loved the lone thing that knew no change
  In the soul of the boy and man.

XI.

And the tears I wept in the wilderness
  And that froze on my lids, did fall,
And melted to pearls for my sinfulness,
  Like scales from the eyes of Paul:
And the last dear thing I was fond to love,
  Was that holy service high,
That lifted my soul to joys above,
  And pleasures that do not die.

XII.

And then, said I, one thing there is
    That I of the LORD desire,
That ever, while I on earth shall live,
    I will of the LORD require,
That I may dwell in His temple blest
    As long as my life shall be,
And the beauty fair of the LORD of Hosts
    In the home of His glory see.

St. Sacrament.

A LEGEND OF LAKE GEORGE.

I.

A SUMMER shower had swept the woods;
But when, from all the scene,
Rolled off at length the thunder-clouds,
And streamed the sunset sheen;
I came where my postilion raised
His horsewhip for a wand,
And said, There's Horicon, good sir,
And here's the Bloody Pond!

II.

And don't you see yon low gray wall,
  With grass and bushes grown?
Well, that's Fort George's palisade,
  That many a storm has known:
But here's the Bloody Pond, where sleeps
  Full many a soldier tall;
The spring, they say, was never pure
  Since that red burial.

III.

'Twas rare to see! That vale beneath;
  That lake so calm and cool!
But mournful was each lily-wreath
  Upon the turbid pool:
And—on, postilion, let us haste
  To greener banks, I cried,
Oh, stay me not where man has stained
  With brother's blood the tide!

IV.

An hour—and though the Even-star
  Was chasing down the sun,
My boat was on thine azure wave,
  Sweet, holy Horicon!

And woman's voice cheered on our bark,
  With soft bewildering song,
While fire-flies darting through the dark
  Went lighting us along.

        V.

Anon, that bark was on the beach,
  And soon, I stood alone
Upon thy mouldering walls, Fort George,
  So old, and ivy-grown.
At once, old tales of massacre
  Were crowding on my soul,
And ghosts of ancient sentinels
  Paced up the rocky knoll.

        VI.

The shadowy hour was dark enow
  For fancy's wild campaign,
And moments were impassioned hours
  Of battle and of pain;
Each brake and thistle seemed alive
  With fearful shapes of fight,
And up the feather'd scalp-locks rose
  Of many a tawny sprite.

VII.

The Mohawk war-whoop howled agen
    I heard St. Denys' charge,
And then the volleyed musketry
    Of England and St. George.
The vale, the rocks, the cradling hills,
    From echoing rank to rank,
Rung back the warlike rhetoric
    Of Huron and of Frank.

VIII.

So, keep thy name, Lake George, said I,
    And bear to latest day,
The memory of our primal age,
    And England's early sway;
And when Columbia's flag shall here
    Her starry glories toss,
Be witness how our fathers fought
    Beneath St. George's cross.

IX.

An hour again—and shone the moon
    Above the mountain gray,
And there the pearly Horicon
    Leap'd up like fountain spray;

The rippled wavelets seemed to dance,
   And starlight seemed to sing;
I never saw, in all my life,
   So gay and bright a thing.

X.

And nought, save lulling Katydid,
   Presumed the hush to mar;
And then it was, I longed to hear
   Some light canoe afar;
I listened for the paddle's dip,
   And in the moon-path clear,
I wished some Indian bark might glide,
   With all its shapes of fear.

XI.

The Indian tales of Horicon
   Were in my spirit now,
And Sachems of the olden time,
   With more than Roman brow;
And all the forest histories
   That make our young romance,
As in a wizard's glass, they moved
   O'er that blue lake's expanse.

XII.

And keep thy name, clear Horicon,
    Thine Indian name, said I;
'Tis meet, if thine old lords are dead,
    Their fame should never die:
So keep thy name, sweet Horicon,
    And be, to latest days,
Thine old free-dwellers' monument,
    Their glory and their praise.

XIII.

But morn was up, the beamy morn,
    That sapphire lake above,
O'er waters blue as amethyst,
    And innocent as love;
And there 'twas glorious to cool
    The glowing breast and limb,
For never did a river-nymph
    In sweeter ripples swim.

XIV.

All day my boat was on the lake,
    My thoughts upon its shore;
And emerald islets, one by one,
    My joyous footsteps bore:

And where, 'mid green and mossy nests,
  The sparks of quartz outshine,
I pulled young flowerets from the rocks,
  And oped the crystal mine.

XV.

But when the breezy even came,
  Again, outstretched I lay,
Upon the weedy battlements
  Of that old ruin gray.
And all alone, 'twas beautiful
  To muse, reclining there,
And feel the chill, so desolate,
  Of half autumnal air.

XVI.

Afar, afar, I cast mine eye
  Adown the winding view:
The lake, the distance, and the sky,
  Were all a heavenly blue:
And distant THUNG rose glorious
  With colours for his crown,
And girt with clouds all rainbow-like,
  And robes of green and brown.

XVII.

A holy stillness, and a calm,
   O'er me and nature stole,
And like a babe the waters slept
   Within their pebbled bowl:
The gales that tossed my tangled hair,
   And stirred the fragrant fern,
They only kissed the water's breast,
   And smoothed its brimming urn.

XVIII.

And I was dreaming, though awake,
   Such thoughts as made me sigh,
When, hark! the alder-bushes break,
   And falls a footstep nigh!
A man of olden years came up;
   A brown old yeoman he,
And on, through thorn and reedy bank,
   He pushed his way to me.

XIX.

He climbed the rough old demilune,
   With iron-studded shoe,
Upturning, at his every stride,
   Old flints and bullets too.

And arrow-heads that told a tale
  Were in each earthy clod
That rumbled down the ravelin,
  And crumbled as he trod.

XX.

Now tell me, tell me, yeoman good,
  One tale to bear away,
With relics for the well-beloved,
  Of this old ruin gray;
With flowers I've gathered round the mole,
  One legend would I twine;
And you may chance remember one
  That was some kin of mine!

XXI.

Canst tell of Cleveland, or Monroe,
  That fought for George's sake;
Or know you of the young Montcalm,
  Or Uncas—on the lake?
He called it Lake St. Sacrament,
  That yeoman brown and brave,
And thus, half soldier and half hind,
  His simple story gave:

XXII.

My father was a Frenchman bold,
    Came o'er the bitter sea,
And here he poured his red heart's blood
    For Louis' fleur-de-lys :
And yonder did he bid me swear
    To say, when he was gone,
He drinks the Holy Sacrament
    Who drinks of Horicon.

XXIII.

And then a lake-drop on his lip,
    A tear-drop in his eye,
He blest his boy, his king, his GOD,
    And turned his face to die :
A moment—and St. George's flag,
    And England's musket roar,
They rapt me from my soldier-sire,
    And I beheld no more.

XXIV.

He drinks the Holy Sacrament
    Who drinks this crystal wave,
That Sacrament baptized his death,
    And was, they say, his grave :

Adieu, adieu, thou stranger youth,
　But say, when I am gone,
This lake is Lake St. Sacrament,
　And not Lake Horicon.

XXV.

And down the quarry stumbled he,
　Ere I could hold him back;
But sounds of crackling alder-bush
　Betrayed his sturdy track.
I saw the cottage-smoke upwreathe
　Beneath the mountain shade,
And there I knew that old yeoman
　His hermitage had made.

XXVI.

And there, when I had followed him,
　He told me more and more,
The magic and the witchery
　Of that romantic shore.
'Tis many a year, he said, since here
　There was no Christian soul;
The Indian only, or the deer,
　To taste these waters stole.

XXVII.

The savage, in the heat of noon,
    Came panting through the wood
To stain the silver-pebbled beach,
    And wash away his blood:
And there, where those tall aspens stand
    They fought a horrid fray;
The very leaves that shaded them
    Are trembling to this day.

XXVIII.

But years rolled on—the sun beheld
    Those savage chiefs agen,
All gathered as at council fires,
    Or leagued with peaceful men:
They listed in their multitudes,
    To one, that midst them stood,
And reared the Cross—as painters draw
    John Baptist in the Wood.

XXIX.

They listened to his wondrous words
    Upon the pebbled strand;
And ay—they welcomed in their hearts,
    The reign of God at hand.

With laud and anthem rung the grove;
  And here, where howled their yell,
I've heard their Christian litanies,
  And high TE DEUM swell.

XXX.

And when the golden Easter came
  Again they gathered there,
All eager for the Christian name,
  And CHRIST's dear Cross to bear.
Oh! forest-aisles, ye trembled then,
  Like fanes where organs roll,
To hear those savage-featured men
  Outpour the Christian soul.

XXXI.

And in the wild-wood's walks they knelt
  To own their sins and pray;
And in these holy water-floods,
  They washed their sins away:
By Horicon, the Trinal GOD
  Confessed them for His sons,
And here the HOLY SPIRIT sealed
  His own begotten ones.

XXXII.

Oh! Abana and Pharpar old
    Must yield to Jordan's flow;
But never this clear Horicon;
    The Prophet said not so!
For sins more dire than leprosy
    These waves have washed away,
And so they named clear Horicon,
    St. Sacrament, for aye.

XXXIII.

Then onward sped the missionaire
    The wilderness to wake:
A voice was on the desert air,
    For GOD a highway make!
The lifted Cross, from hill to hill,
    Proclaimed the Gospel word,
But sweet St. Sacrament was still
    The laver of the LORD.

XXXIV.

And years on years went rolling by;
    The Indian boy grew old;
But longed once more, ere he should die,
    That laver to behold:

And panting from his pilgrimage
  He came at heat of day;
The lake was calm as in his youth,
  St. Sacrament, for aye.

XXXV.

Then fell the white man's tracks around
  Upon this virgin sand:
And bowed thy glories, Horicon,
  Before his faithless hand!
He sent these waters o'er the sea
  In marble urns to shine,
And christened babes of royalty
  In streams that christened mine.

XXXVI.

Adieu, adieu! my stranger boy;
  But say, when I am gone,
This lake is Lake St. Sacrament,
  And not Lake Horicon:
And when some lip that charmeth thee
  Shall ask of thee a lay,
Oh bid her call Lake Horicon,
  St. Sacrament, for aye.

XXXVII.

Then keep thy name, sweet Lake, said I,
   Thine holy name alone!
I love St. George's memory,
   And Indian honour flown;
But never heard I history
   Like thine, old man, this day:
The lake is CHRIST's for evermore,
   St. Sacrament, for aye!

Antioch.

And the disciples were called CHRISTIANS first in Antioch.—*Acts of the Apostles.*

I.

OLD Antioch shall answer ye
    What title I would claim!
Old Antioch—whence Christian men
    Confess their Christian name.
I wear no other name but CHRIST's,
    And His is name enow,
Writ by our mother's spousal hand
    On all her children's brow.

II.

Yet something doth that mother give,
  A token to her sons,
And Catholic doth she surname
  Her LORD's begotten ones:
And such, the children of her love
  Are children all of Heaven:
Lo I—she answereth to GOD,
  And these that Thou hast given.

III.

I know that many martyrs died
  At rack and cruel stake,
And Cranmer laid his prelate hand
  On fire, for JESU's sake;
And many a bishop's burning heart,
  Like flame was lost in flame:
But CHRIST—none other died for me;
  I'll wear no other name.

IV.

I wear the name of CHRIST my GOD,
  So name me not from man!
And my broad country Catholic,
  It hath nor tribe nor clan:

And one and endless is the line
  Through all the world that went,
Commissioned from that Holy Hill
  Of Christ's sublime ascent.

v.

For there, our great Melchizedek
  Ordained of God that came,
And not Himself did glorify
  To wear His priestly name,
His mantle—as He went on high,
  To chosen sons bequeathed,
And bade Apostles feed His lambs,
  As o'er them all He breathed.

vi.

'Twas there, as God had sent the Son,
  The Son His own did send,
And with them promised to abide
  For ever—to the end :
And faithful to His plighted love,
  The Lord is with us yet,
Where our apostles bear the keys
  He left on Olivet.

VII.

Then call me not to other folds;
  No greener fields I see;
The shepherds of my LORD alone
  Can feed a lamb like me:
I cannot wander, if I will,
  For whensoever wooed,
Out-flames a burning chronicle
  In Peter and in Jude.

VIII.

I read how Korah boldly swung
  The censer GOD abhorr'd,
And spurned old Aaron's litanies,
  Commanded of the LORD.
Those bold Apostles echo it,
  And while their voice I hear,
If your strange folds seemed Eden's gate
  That waving sword I fear.

IX.

I hear my Saviour's earnest prayer,
  That one we all may be,
And—oh, how can I go with them
  Who tear Him bodily?

I see the heralds of His cross
    Whom Jesus sent of yore;
And can I spurn anointed hands?
    I love my Saviour more.

x.

Dear Lamb of God! I know full well
    All power to Thee was given,
And oh there is no other Name,
    To name us, under heaven!
I know when Thou didst send a line
    Through all the world to run,
No arm of flesh, if that hath failed,
    Can weave a surer one!

xi.

Thou, Priest and Prophet art for us,
    Our great High Priest in heaven;
While to Thy lowly priests on earth,
    Thy prophet voice is given:
Thank God, it never failed, nor shall!
    That long unbroken chain
Begun in Thee—in Thee shall end,
    When Thou shalt come again.

XII.

So CHRIST forbid that I should boast,
    Save in His blood-red cross;
And let me, for the Crucified,
    Count other gain but loss;
And ye that scorn His follower,
    And deem my glory shame,
Forget not, in upbraiding me,
    To name me by His name.

Dreamland.

I.

A LAY, a lay, good Christians!
   I have a tale to tell,
Though I have ne'er a palmer's staff,
   Nor hat with scallop-shell:
And though I never went astray
   From this mine own countree,
I'll tell what never pilgrim told
   That ever rode the sea.

II.

A lay, a lay, good Christians!
   My boyish harp is fain

To chaunt our mother's loveliness,
    In an eternal strain;
And true it is I never strayed
    Beyond her careful hand,
And yet my lay, good Christians,
    Is of a Holy-Land.

III.

In Dreamland once I saw a Church;
    Amid the trees it stood;
And reared its little steeple-cross
    Above the sweet green-wood;
And then I heard a Dreamland chime
    Peal out from Dreamland tower,
And saw how Dreamland Christian-folk
    Can keep the matin-hour.

IV.

And Dreamland Church was decent all,
    And green the churchyard round;
The Dreamland sextons never keep
    Their kine in holy ground:
And not the tinkling cow-bell there
    The poet's walk becalms;
But where the dead in CHRIST repose,
    The bells ring holy psalms.

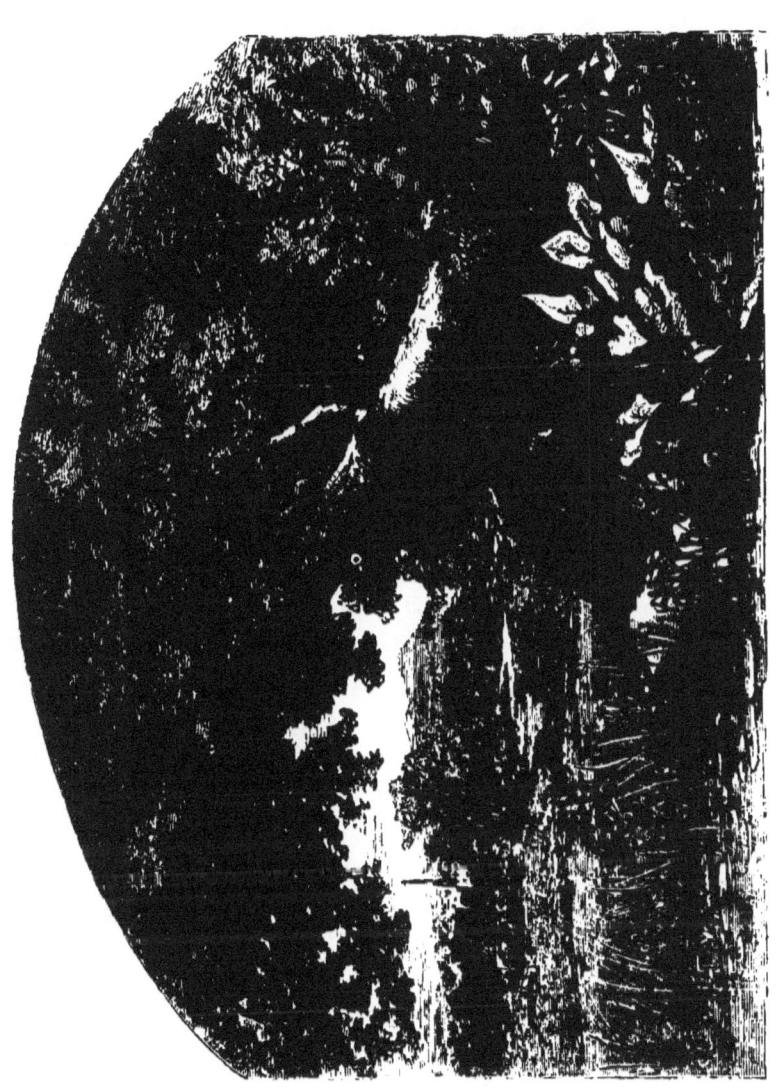

V.

And Dreamland folk do love their dead,
   For every mound I saw,
Had flowers, and wreaths, and garlands, such
   As painters love to draw!
I asked what seeds made such fair buds,
   And—scarce I trust my ears,
The Dreamland folk averred such things
   Do only grow from—tears.

VI.

And while I hung the graves around,
   I heard the organ pour:
I was the only Christian man
   Without that sacred door!
A week-day morn—but church was full;
   And full the chaunting choir,
For Dreamland music is for GOD,
   And not for man and—hire.

VII.

I saw the Dreamland minister
   In snowy vestments pray:
He seemed to think 'twas natural
   That prayer should ope the day:

And Dreamland folk responded loud
   To blessings in GOD's name;
And in the praises of the LORD,
   They had no sense of shame!

VIII.

And Dreamland folk, they kneel them down
   Right on the stony floor;
I saw they were uncivilized,
   Nor knew how we adore:
And yet I taught them not, I own,
   The posture more refined,
For well I knew the picturesque
   Scarce suits the savage mind.

IX.

And Dreamland folk do lowly bow
   To own that CHRIST is GOD:
And I confess I taught them not
   The fashionable nod.
And Dreamland folk sing GLORIA
   At every anthem's close,
But have not learn'd its value yet
   To stir them from a doze.

X.

I saw a Dreamland babe baptized,
    With all the church to see,
And strange as 'twas—the blessed sight
    'Twas beautiful to me!
For many a voice cried loud Amen,
    When, o'er its streaming brow,
The pearly cross was charactered,
    To seal its Christian vow.

XI.

I learned that Dreamland children all,
    As bowing sponsors swear,
To bishop's hands are duly brought,
    To Eucharist and prayer:
And Dreamland maids wear snow-white veils
    At confirmation-hour:
For such—an old Apostle wrote,
    Should clothe their heads, with power.

XII.

The Dreamland folk they wed in church;
    They deem the Lord is there,
And, as of old in Galilee,
    May bless a bridal pair:

And strange enough, the simple ones,
    They see, in wedded love,
Sweet emblems of their Mother Church,
    And CHRIST her LORD above.

XIII.

I saw a Dreamland funeral
    Come up the shadowed way:
The Dreamland priest was surplice-clad
    To meet the sad array;
And when his little flock drew nigh
    To give the dust their dead,
His voice went soothingly before,
    As if a shepherd led.

XIV.

In earth they laid the Dreamland man;
    And then a chaunt was given,
So sweet, that I could well believe,
    I heard a voice from heaven:
And singing children o'er the grave
    Like cherub chaunters stood,
Pouring their angel lullabies,
    To make its slumber good.

XV.

The Dreamland folk count seasons four,
    All woven into one!
'Tis Advent, Lent, or Easter tide,
    Or Trinity begun:
The first is green as emerolde,
    The next of cypress hue,
The third is glorious all as gold,
    The fourth is sapphire-blue.

XVI.

The Dreamland folk are simple ones;
    Who knows but these are they,
Described in ancient chronicle,
    As Children of the Day!
They seemed no denizens of earth,
    But more—a pilgrim band,
With no abiding city here,
    Who seek a better land.

XVII.

So ends my lay, good Christians;
    And ye that gave me ear,
Confess that 'twas of Holy-Land,
    I beckoned ye to hear:

CHRIST bring us all, who bear His cross
Unto His own countree!
And so no more, good Christians,
Of Dreamland, or of me.

Carol.

My Beloved is gone down into His garden, to the beds of spices, to feed in the gardens, and to gather lilies.—*Canticles.*

I.

KNOW—I know
Where the green leaves grow,
   When the woods without are bare;
Where a sweet perfume
Of the woodland's bloom,
   Is afloat on the winter air!
When tempest strong
Hath howled along,
   With his war-whoop wild and loud,

Till the broad ribs broke
Of the forest oak,
   And his crown of glory bowed;
I know—I know
Where the green leaves grow,
   Though the groves without are bare,
Where the branches nod,
Of the trees of GOD,
   And wild vines flourish fair.

II.

For a fragrant crown
When the LORD comes down,
   Of the deathless green we braid,
O'er the altar bright,
Where the tissue white
   Like winter snow is laid,
And we think 'tis meet
The LORD to greet
   As wise men did of old,
With the spiceries
Of incense-trees,
   And hearts like the hoarded gold.
And so we shake
The snowy flake

From cedar and myrtle fair;
And the boughs that nod
On the hills of GOD,
  We raise to His glory there.

III.

I know—I know
Where blossoms blow
  The earliest of the year;
Where the passion-flower
With a mystic power,
  Its thorny crown doth rear;
Where crocus breathes,
And fragrant wreaths
  Like a censer fill the gale;
Where cowslips burst
To beauty first,
  And the lily of the vale:
And snow-drops white;
And pansies bright
  As Joseph's coloured vest;
And laurel-tod
From the woods of GOD,
  Where the wild-bird builds her nest.

IV.

For, oh! we fling
Each fragrant thing
 In the path of the newly-wed;
And, when we weep,
Put flowers to sleep,
 On the breast of the early dead.
And the altar's lawn,
At morning's dawn,
 We deck at Easter-tide,
And the font's fair brim;
To tell of Him
 Who liveth though He died!
Of flowers he spake;
And for His sake
 Whose text was the lilies' bloom,
We search abroad
For the flowers of GOD,
 To give Him their sweet perfume.

V.

I know—I know
Where the waters flow
 In a marble font and nook,

CAROL.

When the frosty sprite
In his strange delight
   Hath fettered the brawling brook;
When the dancing stream
With its broken gleam,
   Is locked in its rocky bed;
And the sing-song fret
Of the rivulet
   Is hush as the melted lead;
Oh then I know
Where the waters flow
   As fresh as the spring-time flood,
When the spongy sod
Of the fields of GOD
   And the hedges are all in bud.

VI.

For the flowing Font
Bids Frost avaunt,
   And the Winter's troop so wild;
And still 'twill gush
In a free full flush,
   At the cry of a little child.
Oh rare the gleam
Of the blessed stream

In the noon of a winter day,
When the ruby stain
Of the coloured pane,
 Falls in, with holy ray!
For then I think
Of the brimming brink,
 And the urns, at the voice divine,
Like Moses' rod
And the rocks of GOD,
 That flushed into ruddy wine.

VII.

I know—I know
No place below,
 Like the home I fear and love;
Like the stilly spot
Where the world is not,
 But the nest of the Holy Dove.
For there broods He
'Mid every tree
 That grows at the Christmas-tide,
And there, all year,
O'er the font so clear,
 His hovering wings abide!
And so, I know
No place below

So meet for the bard's true lay,
As the alleys broad
Of the Church of GOD,
  Where Nature is green for aye.

Lament.

FOR THE LENTEN SEASON.

And of some, have compassion.—*St. Jude.*

I.

O

H weep for them who never knew
    The mother of our love,
And shed thy tears for orphan one
    Whom angels mourn above;
The wandering sheep—the strayin
    lambs,
When wolves were on the wold,
That left our Shepherd's little flock,
And ventured from His fold.

II.

Nay, blame them not! for them the Lord
    Hath loved as well as you:

But oh, like JESUS pray for them
   Who know not what they do :
Oh plead, as once the Saviour did,
   That we may all be One,
That so the blinded world may know
   The Father sent the Son.

III.

Oh let thy Lenten litanies
   Be full of prayer for them !
Oh go ye to the scattered sheep
   Of Israel's parent stem !
Oh keep thy fast for Christendom !
   For CHRIST's dear body mourn ;
And weave again the seamless robe,
   That faithless friends have torn.

IV.

Ye love your dear home-festivals
   With every month entwined ;
Oh weep for those whose sullen hearths
   No Christmas garlands bind !
Those Iceland regions of the Faith
   No changing seasons cheer,
While our sweet paths drop fruitfulness,
   Through all the joyous year.

V.

What though some borealis-beams
    On Arctic night may flare!
Pray God the sunlight of His love
    May rise serenely there.
For fitful flames, oh plead the Lord
    To give His daily ray,
With manna dropped, at morn and eve,
    Along their desert way.

VI.

Oh weep for those, on whom the Lord
    While here below did weep,
Lest grievous wolves should enter in,
    Not sparing of His sheep;
And eat thy bitter herbs awhile,
    That when our Feast is spread,
These too—that gather up the crumbs,
    May eat the children's bread.

Ember-Prayers.

I.

LET out thy soul, and pray!
  Not for thy home alone;
Away in prayer, away!
  Make all the world thine own.
Let out thy soul in prayer;
  Oh, let thy spirit grow!
God gives thee sun and air,
  Let the full blossom blow!

II.

There! dost thou not perceive
  Thy spirit swell within,
And something high receive,
  That is not born of sin?

Oh, paltry is the soul
    That only self can heed!
Sail outward—from the shoal,
    And bourgeon, from the seed!

III.

Rust and the moth consume
    The spangled folds of pride;
Dry-rot doth eat the bloom,
    And gnaw the wealth we hide:
The spirit's selfish care
    Doth die away the same;
But give it air—free air,
    And how the soul can flame!

IV.

Yestreen I did not know
    How largely I could live;
But Faith hath made me grow
    To more than Earth can give.
Joy! for a heart released
    From littleness and pride;
Fast is the spirit's feast,
    And Lent the soul's high tide.

V.

When for the Church I prayed,
   As this dear Lent began,
My thoughts, I'm sore afraid,
   Within small limits ran.
By Ember-week I learned
   How large that prayer might be,
And then, in soul, I burned
   That all might pray with me.

VI.

Plead for the victims all
   Of heresy and sect;
And bow thy knees like Paul,
   For all the LORD's Elect!
Pray for the Church—I mean,
   For Shem and Japhet pray:
And Churches, long unseen,
   In isles, and far away!

VII.

Oh pray that all who err
   May thus be gathered in,
The Moslem worshipper,
   And all the sects of sin!

For all who love in heart,
    But have not found the way,
Pray—and thy tears will start!
    'Twas so the LORD did pray.

VIII.

Now—even for heartless Rome
    Appealing to the LORD,
Be every Church our home,
    And love the battle-word!
The saints' communion—one,
    One Lord—one Faith—one birth,
Oh, pray to GOD the Son,
    For all His Church on Earth.

England.

The glory of children are their fathers.—Proverbs.

I.

AND of the rare old chronicle,
  The legend and the lay,
Where deeds of fancy's dream are truths
  Of all thine ancient day;
Land where the holly-bough is green
  Around the Druid's pile,
And greener yet the histories
  That wreathe his rugged isle;

II.

Land of old story—like thine oak
    The aged, but the strong,
And wound with antique mistletoe
    And ivy-wreaths of song;
Old isle and glorious—I have heard
    Thy fame across the sea,
And know my fathers' homes are thine;
    My fathers rest with thee!

III.

I know they sleep in hallowed ground
    Beneath the church's shade,
Where ring old bells eternally,
    For prayer incessant made.
Nor dull their ear to living prayers,
    Nor vain the anthem's swell;
Where Christian sounds are lulling him,
    The Christian slumbers well.

IV.

And I could yet my dust lay down
    Beneath old England's sward,
For, lulled by her, 'twere sweet to wait
    The coming of the Lord:

Oh England, let thy child desire
    Upon thy breast to be,
And bless thee in the mother-words
    My mother taught to me!

V.

For I have learned them in the tales
    Thy sagest sons have told,
And loved their music in romance
    And roundelays of old:
And I have wooed thy poet tide
    From fountain-head along,
From warbled gush, to torrent roar
    And cataract of song.

VI.

And thou art no strange land to me,
    From Cumberland to Kent,
With hills and vales of household name
    And woods of wild event:
For tales of Guy and Robin Hood
    My childhood ne'er could tire,
And Alfred's poet story roused
    My boyhood to the lyre.

VII.

And I have lived my student years
    On Isis' wizard side,
In sooth, no candidate, I ween,
    For Alma-Mater's pride;
For fancy that could awe my soul
    To surplice, hood, and gown,
Hath mingled me in college freaks,
    And quarrels with the Town.

VIII.

Dear happy homes! where others slight
    The boon my soul had prized,
The cells where sages have been bred,
    And human lore baptized!
Those walks of towering Magdalene
    Those Christ Church meads so fair,
St. Mary's spire—chime answering chime,
    And early bell for prayer!

IX.

Oh shame, ye yawning Baliol men
    Who hate the prayer-bell's toll,
That I, a far-off stranger wight,
    Should love it in my soul;

That oft the Mantuan's hackneyed verse
  Revives at thought of you;
Oh, happiest of the happy—ye,
  If but your bliss ye knew!

X.

In day-dreams of the roving wish,
  The Cherwell's banks I've trod;
Have pulled an oar on Isis' tide,
  Or strayed with gun and rod;
Have taken rooms, burglarious thought!
  Called quiet Corpus mine;
And won a prize; ye double-firsts,
  Forgive the bold design!

XI

It ne'er can be—but, fancy-free,
  To live in one's desire,
To catch from dreams what real life
  In Oxford would inspire;
This use of fancy have I made
  Forbidden else to roam,
Till England is a home to me,
  Besides my native home.

XII.

Fair isle! Thy Dove's wild dale along
    With Walton have I roved,
And London too, with all the heart
    Of burly Johnson, loved:
Chameleon-like, my soul has ta'en
    It every hue from thine,
From Eastcheap's epidemic laugh
    To Avon's gloom divine.

XIII.

All thanks to pencil, and the page
    Of graver's mimic art,
That England's panorama gave
    To picture up my heart;
That round my spirit's eye hath built
    Thine old cathedral piles,
And flung the chequered window-light
    Adown their trophied aisles.

XIV.

I know thine abbey, Westminster,
    As sea-birds know their nest,
And flies my home-sick soul to thee,
    When it would find a rest;

Where princes and old bishops sleep,
  With sceptre and with crook,
And mighty spirits haunt around
  Each Gothic shrine and nook.

XV.

I feel the sacramental hue
  Of choir and chapel, there,
And pictured panes that chasten down
  The day's unholy glare;
And dear it is, on cold gray stone,
  To see the sunbeams crawl,
In long-drawn lines of coloured light
  That streak the bannered wall.

XVI.

I hear the priest's far-dying chaunt,
  The organ's thunder-roll;
I kneel me on the chilly floor,
  And pray with all my soul;
I feel that God Himself is there,
  And saints are sleeping round;
Oh, save the Holy Sepulchre,
  'Tis Earth's most holy ground!

XVII.

Thus, Albion, have I lived with thee,
    Though born so far away;
With thee I spend each holy eve,
    And every festal day.
My Sunday morn is musical,
    With England's steeple-tone;
And when thy Christmas hearths are bright,
    A blaze is on my own.

XVIII.

What though upon thy dear green hills
    My footsteps never trod;
Thine empire is as far and wide
    As all the world of God!
And by the sea-side glorious
    Have I been wont to stand,
For Ocean is old England's own,
    Where'er it beats the land.

XIX.

I've seen thy beacon-banners blaze
    Our mountain coast along,
And swelled my soul with memories
    Of old romaunt and song:

Of Chevy-chase, of Agincourt,
  Of many a field they told;
Of Norman and Plantagenet,
  And all their fame of old!

XX.

What though the red-cross blazonry
  Waved fast and far away;
Not so the flourished vaunt it flung
  Of Cœur-de-Lion's day;
Not so the golden tales it told
  Of crown and kingdom won,
And how my own forefathers fought
  For CHRIST, at Ascalon.

XXI.

And well thy banner-folds may bear
  In red—the Holy Rod,
Thy priests have princes been to men,
  Thy princes, priests to GOD!
And bold to win a crown in heaven
  The Royal Martyr bled;
The martyrs' noble host is full
  Of England's noblest dead.

XXII.

Thy holy Church—the Church of God
  That hath grown old in thee,
Since there the ocean-roving Dove
  Came bleeding from the sea;
When pierced afar, her weary feet
  Could find no home but thine,
Until thine altars were her nest,
  Thy fanes her glory's shrine;

XXIII.

At least that holy Church is mine!
  And every hallowed day,
I bend where England's anthems swell,
  And hear old England pray:
And England's old adoring rites,
  And old liturgic words,
Are mine—but not for England's sake;
  I love them as the LORD's!

XXIV.

And I have sung. By Babel's stream
  The Hebrew's harp was still,
For there, there was no GOD for him,
  No shrine and holy hill:

But here, by Hudson's glorious wave,
   A song of thee I'll sound,
For England's sons and spires are here,
   And England's GOD around.

Chronicles.

I.

THE STORY OF SOME RUINS.

I.

THE abbeys and the arches,
  The old cathedral piles,
Oh, weep to see the ivy
  And the grass in all their aisles;
The vaulted roof is fallen,
  And the bat and owl repose
Where once the people knelt them,
  And the high TE DEUM rose.

II.

Oh, were they not our Father's!
   Was not his honour there!
Or hath the LORD deserted
   His holy House of Prayer!
Time was, when they were sacred
   As the place of Jacob's rest,
And their altars all as spotless
   As the Virgin Mother's breast.

III.

Oh, wo! the hour that brought him,
   The Roman and his reign,
To shed o'er all our temples
   The scarlet hue and stain:
Till the mitre and the crosier
   Were dizen'd o'er with gems,
And sullied with the tinsel
   Of the Cæsars' diadems.

IV.

But still our Father loved us;
   And the Holy Place had still
Its beauty, and its glory,
   On its old eternal hill.

His heritage they trampled,
Those men of iron rod!
But still it towered in honour,
The temple of our God.

II.

MARTYRS REFORM THE CHURCH.

I.

YE abbeys and ye arches,
  Ye old cathedral piles,
The martyrs' noble army
  Are in your hallowed aisles.
And the bishop and the baron
  Have knelt together there,
And breathed a vow to heaven,
  In agony of prayer.

II.

And to chase away the tyrant
  From England's happy home,
They have risen like their fathers,
  'Gainst the cruel hordes of Rome;

For oh they love the temples
    Where virgin Faith has trod,
Though all too long within them
    Man showed himself as God.

III.

Ye abbeys and ye arches,
    Ye old cathedral piles,
Again a holy incense
    Is in your vaulted aisles!
Again in noble English
    The Christian anthems swell,
And out the organ pealeth,
    Over stream and stilly dell.

IV.

And the bishop, and the deacon,
    And the presbyter are there,
In pure and stainless raiment,
    At Eucharist and prayer;
And the bells swing free and merry,
    And a nation shouteth round,
For the Lord Himself hath triumphed,
    And His voice is in the sound.

III.

BUT REGICIDES MAKE DISSENT:

I.

YE abbeys and ye arches,
    Ye old cathedrals blest,
  Be strong against the earthquake,
    And the days of your unrest;
  For not the haughty Roman
Could make old England bow,
But the children of her bosom
  Are the foes that trouble now.

II.

A gleam is in the abbey,
  And a sound ariseth there;
'Tis not the light of worship,
  'Tis not the voice of prayer:

Their hands are red with murder,
    And a prince's fall they sing!
They would slay the Lord of glory
    Should He come again as King.

III.

And a lawless soldier tramples
    Where the holy loved to kneel,
And he spurns a bishop's ashes
    With his ruffian hoof of steel:
Ay, horses have they stabled
    Where the blessed martyrs knelt,
That neigh—where rose the anthem,
    And the psalm that made us melt.

IV.

There, once a glorious window
    Shed down a flood of rays,
With rainbow hues and holy,
    And colours all ablaze:
Its pictured panes are broken,
    Our fathers' tombs profaned,
And the font where we were christened,
    With the blood of brothers stained.

IV.

AND FULFIL THE SEVENTY-FOURTH PSALM.

I.

YE abbeys and ye arches,
   Ye old cathedrals dear,
The hearts that love you tremble,
   And your enemies have cheer;
But the prayers ye heard are breathing,
   And your litanies they sing;
There are holy men in England
   That are praying for their king.

II.

The noble in the cottage,
   While the hind is in his hall,

Still kneels, as if he heard them,
    When your chimes were wont to call:
And at morning, and at evening,
    There are high-born hearts and true,
In the lowliest huts of England,
    That will bless the king, and you.

III.

And bishops, in their prison,
    Will still the Lessons read,
How the good are often troubled,
    While the vilest men succeed:
How God's own heart may honour
    Whom the people oft disown,
And how the royal David
    Was driven from his throne.

IV.

And their Psalter mourneth with them,
    O'er the carvings and the grace,
Which axe and hammer ruin,
    In the fair and holy place;
O'er the havoc they are making
    In all the land abroad,
And the banners of the cruel
    In the dwelling-house of God.

V.

BUT GOD IS WITH US TO THE END.

I.

YE abbeys and ye arches,
    How few and far between,
The remnants of your glory
    In all their pride are seen!
A thousand fanes are fallen,
    And the bat and owl repose
Where once the people knelt them,
    And the high TE DEUM rose.

II.

But their dust and stones are precious
    In the eyes of pious men,
And the baron hath his manor,
    And the king his own again!
And again the bells are ringing
    With a free and happy sound,
And again TE DEUM riseth
    In all the churches round.

III.

Now pray we for our mother,
    That England long may be
The holy, and the happy,
    And the gloriously free!
Who blesseth her, is blessed!
    So peace be in her walls;
And joy in all her palaces,
    Her cottages and halls!

IV.

All ye who pray in English,
    Pray GOD for England, pray!
And chiefly, thou, my country,
    In thy young glory's day!

Pray God those times return not,
　'Tis England's hour of need!
Pray for thy mother—daughter,
　Plead God for England—plead.

The Chimes of England.

I.

CHIMES, the chimes of Motherland,
 Of England green and old,
That out from fane and ivied tower
 A thousand years have tolled;
How glorious must their music be
As breaks the hallowed day,

And calleth with a seraph's voice
A nation up to pray!

II.

Those chimes that tell a thousand tales,
   Sweet tales of olden time;
And ring a thousand memories
   At vesper, and at prime!
At bridal and at burial,
   For cottager and king,
Those chimes—those glorious Christian chimes,
   How blessedly they ring!

III.

Those chimes, those chimes of Motherland,
   Upon a Christmas morn,
Outbreaking as the angels did,
   For a Redeemer born:
How merrily they call afar,
   To cot and baron's hall,
With holly decked and mistletoe,
   To keep the festival!

IV.

The chimes of England, how they peal
   From tower and gothic pile,

Where hymn and swelling anthem fill
    The dim cathedral aisle ;
Where windows bathe the holy light
    On priestly heads that falls,
And stain the florid tracery
    Of banner-dighted walls!

V.

And then, those Easter bells in Spring,
    Those glorious Easter chimes!
How loyally they hail thee round,
    Old Queen of holy times!
From hill to hill, like sentinels,
    Responsively they cry,
And sing the rising of the LORD,
    From vale to mountain high.

VI.

I love ye—chimes of Motherland,
    With all this soul of mine,
And bless the Lord that I am sprung
    Of good old English line:
And like a son I sing the lay
    That England's glory tells;
For she is lovely to the LORD,
    For you, ye Christian bells!

VII.

And heir of all her olden fame,
   Though far away my birth,
Thee too I love, my Forest-land,
   The joy of all the earth;
For thine thy mother's voice shall be,
   And here—where GOD is King,
With English chimes, from Christian spires,
   The wilderness shall ring.

Scotland.

THE ORANGE SACRILEGE.

Though all the nations that are under the king's dominion obey him and fall away, every one from the religion of their fathers, ... GOD forbid that we should forsake the law, and the ordinances! We will not hearken to the king's words to go from our religion, either on the right hand or the left.—*Maccabees.*

I.

'TWAS a true-hearted Scotsman
 Had risen from his knees,
All in a glorious chapel
 Reared by the old Culdees.
That day the axe of Orange
 On Scotland's altars rung,
And down fair cross and crosier
 Upon the Earth were flung.

II.

And as he rose from praying
 The raving mob broke in;

And as he passed the portal,
   He heard the spoiler's din.
He beat his breast—and tear-drops
   They stood in either eye:
He left that church forever,
   But thus did prophesy.

III.

Ah me—St. Andrew's crosier!
   'Tis broken and laid low:
God help thee, Church of Scotland,
   It seemeth thy death blow!
They've robbed thee of thine altars,
   They've ta'en thine ancient name;
But thou'rt the Church of Scotland
   Till Scotland melts in flame.

IV.

Ay—hear it, heartless William,
   Thou shalt have ne'er a son!
Thy tree—it shall be blighted,
   For this that thou hast done:
Thine orange-bough, in Britain,
   Shall leave nor branch nor shoot,
For God uproots the sovereign
   That would His Church uproot.

V.

Ay—grasp old Scotia's thistle,
    Thy daring hand must bleed:
But touch the cross of Andrew,
    Thy soul shall rue the deed!
Unroof the Church of Scotland,
    She lives in dens and caves;
She cries to GOD, and tyrants
    Are ashes, in their graves.

VI.

And thou, old Church, like princes
    When clowns usurp their state,
Shalt be confest, in exile,
    The ancient and the great!
Not she that thus usurpeth
    Can boast one grace of thine;
That grace—it cometh only
    Of Apostolic line.

VII.

Then leave to grim Genevans
    Cathedral choir and aisle,
Let psalms of Covenanters
    Be quavered there awhile!

The very stones shall flout them,
    In beauty built, and might,
For apostolic service,
    And high liturgic rite.

VIII.

And thou, true Church of Scotland,
    Cast down, shalt not despair;
When dowered wives are barren,
    The desolate shall bear;
Thy sons—they shall be princes,
    To take their fathers' stead,
And shame the Church whose portion
    Is proud, and full of bread.

IX.

When o'er the western waters
    They seek for crook and key,
The LORD shall make like Hannah's
    Thy poor and low degree!
Thou o'er new worlds the sceptre
    Of Shiloh shalt extend,
And see a line of children
    From thy sad breast descend.

X.

And when, at length, old Scotland,
   Her chiefs and her true men,
Her Highlands and her Lowlands
   Shall find their hearts agen:
When martyr'd Sharpe upriseth
   In spirit 'gainst his foes,
And souls are bred in Scotland
   To match the great Montrose;

XI.

In Edin's high cathedral,
   No more the fish-wife's voice;
In Glasgow's crypts and cloisters,
   No more the rabble's choice;
Oh then St. Andrew's crosier
   Once more shall be upheld,
And the Culdee mitre glisten
   In Brechin and Dunkeld.

XII.

See after See uprearing
   Once more the shattered cross;
Once more a bishop treading
   The heathery braes of Ross;

Fair Elgin's choir enfolding
  The Moray shepherd's rest,
And Holyrood—from ruins
  Uprising, bright and blest;

XIII.

From Berwick to the Orkneys,
  How each old kirk shall gleam
In beauty and in brightness,
  With thy returning beam!
One heart in Gael and Saxon,
  In cotter and in thane;
One creed—one Church in Scotland,
  From Caithness to Dumblane!

XIV.

Then faint not, Church of Scotland!
  Thy beauty and thy worth
Shall make a new uprising,
  In fair and sightly Perth;
When shines in wild Glenalmond
  The dew of thy new day,
Again thy noon of glory
  Shall glitter o'er the Tay.

XV.

Bide thou thy time in patience!
The sons of thy bold foes
Shall build thine old waste places,
Dunfermline and Melrose.
Where now the sons of havoc
Upon thine altars tread,
Thine own Liturgic Service
Shall bless the Cup and Bread.

XVI.

Save only from the spoiler
That pure and ancient rite!
In Scotland's pure Oblation
All churches must unite:
And—as the Ark of Scotland,
Keep thou thy rightful name,
For thou'rt the Church of Scotland
Till Scotland melts in flame!

Seabury's Mitre:

IN TRINITY COLLEGE, HARTFORD.

I.

HE rod that from Jerusalem
   Went forth so strong of yore;
That rod of David's royal stem,
   Whose hand the farthest bore?
St. Paul to seek the setting sun,
   They say, to Britain prest:
St. Andrew to old Caledon;
   But who still further West?

II.

Go ask!—a thousand tongues shall tell
   His name and dear renown,

Where altar, font, and holy bell,
    Are gifts he handed down:
A thousand hearts keep warm the name,
    Which share those gifts so blest;
Yet even this may tell the same,
    First mitre of the West!

III.

This mitre with its crown of thorn,
    Its cross upon the front;
Not for a proud adorning worn,
    But for the battle's brunt:
This helmet—with Salvation's sign,
    Of one whose shield was faith;
This crown—of him, for right divine
    Who battled unto death!

IV.

Oh! keep it—till the moth shall wear
    Its comeliness to dust,
Type of a crown that's laid up where
    There is nor moth nor rust;
Type of the LORD's commission given
    To this, our Western shore;
The rod of CHRIST—the keys of heaven,
    Through one, to thousands more.

V.

They tell how Scotia keeps with awe
    Her old Regalia bright,
Sign of her independent law,
    And proud imperial right;
But keep this too for Scotland's boast;
    'Twill tell of better things,
When long old Scotia shall have lost
    Those gewgaws of her kings.

VI.

And keep it for this mighty West
    Till truth shall glorious be,
And good old Samuel's is confest
    Columbia's primal see.
'Tis better than a diadem,
    The crown that bishop wore,
Whose hand the rod of David's stem
    The furthest Westward bore.

Rustic Churches.

ST. GABRIEL'S, WINDSOR, CONNECTICUT.

I.

YES—'tis the village-joiner's work,
    With but his axe and saw:
No Wykeham was the humble clerk
    That such a plan could draw!
'Tis what a rural parish could,
    With what its farms supplied;
Not what in mind and heart they would,
    Had they the gold beside.

II.

Yet hath it merit—in the eye
    That can, by fancy's aid,
What time can only give, supply,
    Of shrubbery and shade.

Add but of ancient elms a score,
   Those undissenting trees,
And he that passeth by shall pore,
   Well-pleased, on what he sees.

III.

Its merit, first, is—what 'tis not;
   That hippogriff of art,
By crude Genevan rites begot,
   Half temple, and half mart:
Nor yet that type of changing shifts,
   A hall low-roofed and tinn'd
On which a wooden Babel lifts
   Its weather-cock to wind.

IV.

Nor does it bring those shaggy curs
   Instinctively to mind,
With forward parts adorned in furs,
   But shaven close behind;
Like many a pine-wood parody
   Of Parthenon or Pnyx,
Which oft, as frontispiece, we see,
   To chapel built of bricks.

V.

Again—as country parsons speak,
    Some merit it may claim
In that it dares to look antique,
    In colour and in frame.
And then, no passer-by can doubt
    Its spiritual kin,
For oh, it tells the truth, without,
    Of what it is, within!

VI.

All that the Church requires it hath,
    Chancel, and porch, and nave,
A sacristy, and holy bath
    The sinner's soul to lave:
And in the baptist'ry, a well;
    O'er-head, an open roof;
A gable-cot to hold the bell;
    The cross—a church's proof!

VII.

So once—where now St. Joseph's thorn
    Blooms by an abbey's towers,
Stood the poor Briton's church, forlorn,
    And ruder far than ours!

Nor here the faithful eye shall fail
   The brightening view to catch,
That opened from that structure frail
   Of wicker-work and thatch.

VIII.

For dear is even the first rude art
   Which holy Faith inspires!
The whole is augured from the part,
   Achievements—from desires.
At least such churches symbolize
   The place where CHRIST was born;
And mangers may to minsters rise,
   As noontide from the morn.

In Memoriam

Churchyards.

ST. GEORGE'S, HEMPSTEAD.

I.

NEVER can see a churchyard old,
    With its mossy stones and mounds,
And green-trees weeping the unforgot
    That rest in its hallowed bounds;
I never can see the old churchyard,
    But I breathe to God a prayer,
That, sleep as I may in this fevered life,
    I may rest when I slumber there.

II.

Our mother, the Earth, hath a cradle-bed
    Where she gathereth sire and son,
And the old-world's fathers are pillowed there,
    Her children, every one.

And her cradle it hath a dismal name,
    When riseth the banquet's din,
And pale is the cheek at dance or wine,
    If a song of its sleep break in.

III.

But our mother the Church hath a gentle nest,
    Where the LORD's dear children lie,
And its name is sweet to a Christian ear,
    As a motherly lullaby.
Oh the green churchyard, the green churchyard
    Is the couch she spreads for all;
And she layeth the cottager's baby there,
    With the lord of the tap'stry hall.

IV.

Our mother the Church hath never a child
    To honour before the rest,
But she singeth the same for mighty kings
    And the veriest babe on her breast;
And the bishop goes down to his narrow bed
    As the ploughman's child is laid,
And alike she blesseth the dark-browed serf
    And the chief in his robe arrayed.

V.

She sprinkles the drops of the bright new-birth
  The same on the low and high,
And christens their bodies with dust to dust,
  When earth with its earth must lie;
Oh the poor man's friend is the Church of CHRIST
  From birth to his funeral day;
She makes him the LORD's, in her surpliced arms,
  And singeth his burial lay.

VI.

And ever the bells in the green churchyard
  Are tolling, to tell ye this;
Go pray in the church, while pray ye can,
  That so ye may sleep in bliss.
And wise is he in the glow of life,
  Who weaveth his shroud of rest,
And graveth it plain on his coffin-plate,
  That the dead in CHRIST are blest.

VII.

I never can see a green churchyard
  But I think I may slumber there,
And I wonder within me what strange disease
  Shall bring me to homes so fair;

And whether in breast, in brain, or blood,
  There lurketh a secret sore,
Or whether this heart, so warm and full,
  Hath a worm at its inmost core.

VIII.

For I know, ere long, some limb of mine
  To the rest may traitor prove,
And steal, from the strong young frame I wear,
  The generous flush I love:
I know I may burn into ashes soon,
  With this feverish flame of life;
Or the flickering lamp may soon blaze out,
  With its dying self at strife.

IX.

And here—I think—when they lay me down
  How strange will my slumber be,
The cold cold clay for my dreamless head,
  And the turf for my canopy;
How stilly will creep the long long years
  O'er my quiet sleep away,
And oh what a waking that sleep shall know,
  At the peal of the Judgment-day!

X.

Up—up from the graves and the clods around
  The quickened bones will stare;
I know that within this green churchyard
  A host shall be born to air;
A thousand shall struggle to earth agen,
  From under the sods I tread:
Oh, strange—thrice strange, shall the story be
  Of the field where they lay the dead!

XI.

Oh bury me, then, in the green churchyard,
  As my old forefathers rest,
Nor lay me in cold Necropolis,
  'Mid many a grave unblest;
I would sleep where the church-bells aye ring out;
  I would rise by the house of prayer,
And feel me a moment at home, on earth,
  For the Christian's home is there.

XII.

I never loved cities of living men,
  And towns of the dead I hate;
Oh let me rest in the churchyard then,
  And hard by the church's gate;

'Tis there I pray to my Saviour CHRIST
  And I will, till mine eye is dim,
That, sleep as I may in this fevered life,
  I may rest, at last, in Him.

Trinity, Old Church.

EASTER EVEN, 1840.

Thy servants think upon her stones, and it pitieth them to see her in the dust.—*Psalter*.

I.

THE Paschal moon is ripe to-night
　　On fair Manhada's bay,
And soft it falls on Hoboken,
　　As where the Saviour lay:
　　And beams, beneath whose paly shine
Nile's troubling angel flew,
Show many a blood-besprinkled door
　　Of our Passover too.

II.

But here where, many a holy year,
　　It shone on arch and aisle,

What means its cold and silver ray
    On dust, and ruined pile?
Oh where's the consecrated porch,
    The sacred lintel where,
And where's that antique steeple's height,
    To bless the moonlight air?

III.

I seem to miss a mother's face
    In this her wonted home;
And linger in the green churchyard
    As round that mother's tomb.
Old Trinity! thou too art gone!
    And in thine own blest bound,
They've laid thee low, dear mother church,
    To rest in holy ground!

IV.

The vaulted roof that trembled oft
    Above the chaunted psalm;
The quaint old altar where we owned
    Our very Paschal Lamb;
The chimes that ever in the tower
    Like seraph-music sung,
And held me spell-bound in the way,
    When I was very young;

v.

The marble monuments within;
    The 'scutcheons, old and rich;
And one bold bishop's effigy
    Above the chancel-niche;
The mitre and the legend there
    Beneath the coloured pane;
All these—thou knewest, Paschal moon,
    But ne'er shalt know again!

vi.

And thou wast shining on this spot
    That hour the Saviour rose!
But oh, its look, that Easter morn,
    The Saviour only knows.
A thousand years—and 'twas the same,
    And half a thousand more;
Old moon, what mystic chronicles
    Thou keepest, of this shore!

vii.

And so till good queen Anna reign'd,
    It was a heathen sward:
But then they made its virgin turf
    An altar to the LORD.

With holy roof they covered it;
  And when apostles came,
They claimed, for CHRIST, its battlements,
  And took it, in GOD's Name.

VIII.

Then, Paschal moon, this sacred spot
  No more thy magic felt,
Till flames brought down the holy place
  Where our forefathers knelt.
Again, 'tis down—the grave old pile;
  That mother church sublime!
Look on its roofless floor, old moon,
  For 'tis thy last—last time!

IX.

Ay, look with smiles, for never there
  Shines Paschal moon agen,
Till breaks the Earth's great Easter day
  O'er all the graves of men!
So wane away, old Paschal moon,
  And come next year as bright;
Eternal rock shall welcome thee,
  Our faith's devoutest light!

X.

They rear old Trinity once more :
   And, if ye weep to see,
The glory of this latter house,
   Thrice glorious shall be !
Oh lay its deep foundations strong,
   And, yet a little while,
Our Paschal Lamb Himself shall come
   To light its hallowed aisle.

Trinity, New Church.

ASCENSION DAY, 1846.

I will lay thy stones with fair colours, and lay thy foundations with sapphires. And I will make thy windows of agates and thy gates of carbuncles, and all thy borders of pleasant stones. And all thy children shall be taught of the LORD; and great shall be the peace of thy children.—*Isaiah.*

I.

IS raised in beauty from the dust,
 And 'tis a goodly pile!
So takes our infant Church, I trust,
 Her own true stamp and style.
As birds put forth their own attire,
 As shells o'er sea-nymphs grow,
'Tis ours—nave, chancel, aisle, and spire,
 And not a borrowed show.

II.

Not this, a church without—to hide
  Conventicle within;
Here is no masquerade outside
  Of but the lion's skin!
Not this a lie engraved in rocks!
  'Tis—what it shews abroad,
A mountain piled in shapely blocks,
  And made the House of God.

III.

'Tis native comeliness! As earth
  Puts forth her golden sheaves,
As flowers mature their brilliant birth
  And trees put on their leaves;
As human flesh grows sound and fair
  Around the human bone,
So doth the Church this glory wear,
  And clothe herself in stone.

IV.

How like herself our mother seems
  In this—her ancient dress!
'Tis as a robe the gazer deems
  Well worn by loveliness.

The clothing that befits a queen,
   With ease and grace she wears :
Her home attire, for daily scene,
   And daily work of prayers!

v.

Not this a Gothic gazing stock,
   Where nought is meant or told;
Translated into solid rock,
   The prayer-book's self behold!
Sermons in stones! Yes—more beside,
   A language, and a voice!
Much uttered—but far more implied
   That makes the heart rejoice.

vi.

Without—each little carving speaks
   Of CHRIST, the Crucified,
To Jews a stumbling-block, to Greeks
   'Tis foolishness beside:
But oh, to all the faithful—see,
   From porch to topmost tower,
It telleth of the TRINITY,
   And preacheth CHRIST with power!

VII.

Within—behold the promised grace,
    Fair stones, and colours too,
To beautify the holy place,
    And shed a feeling through!
Windows of agates—pictured sights
    With floral borders bound,
Yes—pleasant stones, and sapphire lights
    That throw a glory round.

VIII.

Oh God, how beautiful and vast
    Men's minds and fancies grow,
When, in Thy mould of doctrine cast,
    Their warm ideas flow:
When 'tis Thy Church inspires the thought,
    And forms the bold design,
Till, from a sullen rock, is wrought
    A symbol so divine!

IX.

But note the better part, as well:
    The Church's children all,
Called daily, by the holy bell,
    To prayer and festival.

Oh gather them from far abroad;
  Oh pray and never cease:
When all thy sons are taught of GOD,
  How great shall be their peace!

X.

Dear cross! hold fast thy height in air:
  Stand ever wide, blest door!
And ever crowd, ye faithful, there,
  High, lowly, rich, and poor!
Sweet bells! ring ever your glad sound,
  And let its message be
Ho! ye that thirst—here CHRIST is found,
  And here His home is free.

The Spire-Cross.

The offence of the Cross.—*St. Paul.*

I.

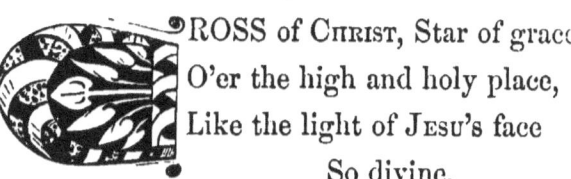ROSS of CHRIST, Star of grace,
O'er the high and holy place,
Like the light of JESU's face
    So divine,
For love of what thou art,
My best and chosen part,
I hail thee in my heart;
    Blessed Sign!

II.

Let Japanese and Jews,
And Antichristian crews,
The stumbling-block refuse
    And deride!
But oh thou glorious Tree,
Bathed with JESU's blood, for me,
Thou Cross of Calvary,
    Crimson dyed:

III.

Their souls have never known
What comes by thee alone,
And their heart is like a stone
    In their breast!
But mine the broken Bread,
And the Blood my SAVIOUR shed;
And the Cross, on which He bled,
    Is my rest.

IV.

How glorious is its form,
In the starlight or the storm,
In the morning, or the warm
    Light of noon;

It peereth in the air,
O'er the holy place of prayer,
And is beautiful and fair,
  By the moon.

v.

Let it be the Christian's boast;
Let it glitter from the coast!
Like a watchman, at his post,
  Let it say—
Here the Lord Jehovah dwells,
Here ring the holy bells,
Here the Church's service swells;
  Come and pray!

vi.

As the rent and ravelled rag
Of the soldier's flying flag,
On the rampart's blazing crag,
  Rouseth him;
It points me to the prize,
And to see it in the skies,
Brings the tear-drops to my eyes,
  And they swim.

VII.

Like a trumpet's stirring psalm,
It reminds me what I am,
A soldier of the Lamb!
   And, right down,
My soul it yearns to kneel,
And renew my SAVIOUR's seal
That I may, with newer zeal,
   Win His crown.

VIII.

And so, thou glorious Cross,
On the steeple's golden boss,
O'er a world of gilded dross,
   Lifted high,
Thou hast been to me, this day,
Like a far descending ray,
That lights some hut of clay,
   From the sky!

IX.

My banner bright art thou,
And I wear thee on my brow,
With my baptismal vow,
   Writ in gore:

Oh JESU, from my heart,
Let its shadow ne'er depart,
But, to bring me where Thou art,
Go before!

Oratories.

PRIVATE PRAYER IN CHURCHES.

I.

IN a church's aisle or towers,
    Vestry, porch, or chancel-side,
If—in prayerless days like ours
    Any open door is spied;
Say not that the Sacristan
    Happens there to ply his broom;
Say—some viewless friend of man
    Beckons thee, and says there's room.
    'Tis the house of prayer—Go in!
    'Tis the Christian's home by right!
    Find some nook, confess thy sin,
    And go forth in JESU's might.

II.

Halt not for some foolish doubt!
  Is it not thy Father's home?
Who will dare to turn thee out,
  When the Master bids thee come?
Is it open? Worship God!
  If another lounges round,
Talking, staring, laughing broad,
  Let him learn—'tis hallowed ground.
    'Tis the house of prayer—&c.

III.

Like the publican of old,
  Hide the face, and smite the breast,
Say his words, and—manifold
  Be thy secret sins confessed!
For the people there that pray,
  For the priest, whose vows are there,
Brother-like a collect say,
  Pray some dear familiar prayer.
    'Tis the house of prayer—&c.

IV.

Oh 'tis sweet a home to claim
  Thus, where'er a church we see,

Stealing in, though not with shame,
   Yet to worship, noiselessly;
Like the birds to nestle there
   Where the Psalmist's cedars grow;
And to leave a fragrant prayer
   Wafting heavenward as we go.
      'Tis the house of prayer—Go in!
      'Tis the Christian's home by right!
      Find some nook—confess thy sin,
         And go forth in JESU's might.

Wayside Homes.

I.

A S I rode on my errand along,
    I came where a prim little spire
Chimed out to the landscape a song,
    And glowed in the sunset like fire.

II.

Its cross beamed a beckoning ray,
    And the home of my Mother I knew;
So I pressed to its portal to pray,
    And my book from my bosom I drew.

III.

How sweet was the service within,
    And the plain rustic chaunt how sincere!

How welcome the pardon of sin,
    And the kind parting blessing how dear!

IV.

And the parson—I knew not his name,
    And the brethren—each face was unknown;
But the Church and the prayers were the same,
    And my heart claimed them all for its own.

V.

For I knew—in my own little nook,
    That eve, the same Psalter was said,
And Lessons, the same from the Book,
    By my far-away darlings were read.

VI.

So I prayed, and went on in my way,
    Blessing GOD for the Church He hath given;
My steed on his journey was gay;
    So was I—on my journey to Heaven.

Little Woodmere.

THE PRAYER-BOOK PATTERN.

I.

NAVE it had and a chancel,
    The Church of Little Woodmere!
A porch at the south: on the north side
    Did a tower and its steeple peer.

II.

And a bell, o'er the eastern gable,
    In a cross-topped belfry swung;
When the Litany was beginning,
    The gable-bell was rung.

III.

The chancel it had a window,
　All cunningly set with stains:
There were angels and saints and martyrs
　Seen in its pictured panes.

IV.

From the dust and noise of the highway,
　'Twas a furlong perchance withdrawn;
Hard by stood the rectory mansion,
　On a trim little shrubbery lawn.

V.

And all round the church was a churchyard,
　With beautiful clumps of trees;
The churchyard cross was planted
　On a hillock—like Calvary's.

VI.

A quaint little roof o'er the gateway,
　Where funerals paused with the bier!
When the priest came forth, in his surplice
　He began the service here.

VII.

The rich and poor, all together,
  On the south of the church were sown,
To be raised in the same incorruption
  When the trumpet, at last, is blown.

VIII.

On the north of the church were buried
  The dead of a hapless fame ;
A cross and a wail for pity,
  But never a date, or name.

IX.

Here and there was a quiet corner,
  With a rustic seat in shade,
Where mourners would come and ponder
  On the dear ones around them laid.

X.

And there I mused till the bell tolled,
  And thought, with the soul in bliss,
The best of good things for the body
  Were to sleep in a spot like this.

XI.

As I joined in the throng from the village
    That were keeping St. Barthelmy's day,
And passed along, with glad faces,
    And festival greetings so gay;

XII.

I was ware of a train of dear children;
    The school of the parish stood near,
And, led by a dame and a deacon,
    They came—full of joy and of fear.

XIII.

And each had a musical Psalter,
    For these were the singers; each one
I fancied might stand for the cherubs
    They carve with a scroll, upon stone.

XIV.

As I entered the nave, by the portal,
    I came to the font, and thought
Of the door to the Church Universal,
    And how the new-birth is wrought.

XV.

For a moment I knelt in devotion;
    And then—as I raised mine eyes
And caught the clear blaze of the chancel
    In the glow of a broad sunrise;

XVI.

The altar—all bright with its silver,
    And the fair white cloth bespread;
The credence prepared for oblation,
    The chalice, and paten of bread;

XVII.

I thought of the Church triumphant,
    And the altar where JESUS stands,
Our great High-Priest for ever,
    With a censer of gold in His hands.

XVIII.

There was a plain cross o'er the rood-loft,
    By the chancel's depth relieved;
And figures were carved, in the railing,
    Of saints who have fought and achieved.

XIX.

And I thought of the happy departed,
  And of Jesu's descent into hell;
And of babes, and of glorious virgins,
  In Paradise-glory that dwell.

XX.

The nave it was dim, for its ceiling
  Was dark with its timbers of oak:
Of the Militant Church 'twas the symbol;
  And here knelt the worshipping folk.

XXI.

They knelt—rich and poor knelt together,
  The ploughman at side of the squire:
They recked not of gewgaw nor feather,
  If white was the soul's attire.

XXII.

On the gospel-side hung the pulpit;
  'Twas carved with an angel and scroll:
And now—from the sacristy entered
  The priest, in his cope and his stole.

XXIII.

And soon swelled the tones of the service:
    The people were singers, each one;
They chaunted a psalm from the Psalter,
    Men and maidens, the sire and the son.

XXIV.

And then came the Prayer and Commandments,
    The Collect, with fervour devout,
And then the Epistle and Gospel;
    And the Creed—it went up with a shout!

XXV.

I would you had listened the sermon:
    Nathanael, the saint without guile,
Was the text—and the blessed example,
    And guileless as he was the style.

XXVI.

And oh, how like Heaven was communion,
    Thus far from the world and its cares!
If my life were but led in that village,
    'Twould indeed be a life-time of prayers.

XXVII.

Afar from the blast of polemics,
   Afar from their hate and their strife,
No scorn of the brawling declaimer
   Should turn the still course of my life.

XXVIII.

While they would rail on, I'd be praying;
   And, blest with a foretaste of bliss,
Live only with Herbert and Ferrar,
   Forgetting such ages as this.

XXIX.

With names, in the Canon of Heaven,
   That shine like the glittering skies,
Mine too be the scorn of the creatures
   Whose god is the Father of Lies;

XXX.

But call me a Jew or a Pagan,
   I'd pray the good LORD to forgive,
And in heart, and in spirit, a Christian,
   'Tis so I would die, and would live.

Desolations.

VIRGINIA CHURCHES.

Jerusalem lieth waste, and the gates thereof are burned with fire; come and let us build up the wall of Jerusalem, that we be no more a reproach. —*Nehemiah.*

I.

AST been where the full-blossomed bay-tree is blowing,
With odours like Eden's around?
Hast seen where the broad-leaved palmetto is growing,
And wild vines are fringing the ground?

Hast sat in the shade of catalpas, at noon,
    To eat the cool gourds of their clime;
Or slept where magnolias were screening the moon,
    And the mocking-bird sung his sweet rhyme?

II.

And didst mark, in thy journey, at dew-dropping eve,
    Some ruin peer high o'er thy way,
With rooks wheeling round it, and ivy to weave
    A mantle for turrets so gray?
Did ye ask if some lord of the cavalier kind
    Lived there, when the country was young?
And burned not the blood of a Christian to find
    How there the old prayer-bell had rung?

III.

And did ye not glow, when they told ye—the LORD
    Had dwelt in that thistle-grown pile;
And that bones of old Christians were under its sward,
    That once had knelt down in its aisle?
And had ye no tear-drops your blushes to steep
    When ye thought—o'er your country so broad,
The bard seeks in vain for a mouldering heap
    Save only these churches of GOD!

IV.

Oh ye that shall pass by those ruins agen,
    Go kneel in their alleys and pray,
And not till their arches have echoed amen
    Rise up, and fare on, in your way.
Pray GOD that those aisles may be crowded once more,
    Those altars surrounded and spread,
While anthems and prayers are upsent as of yore,
    As they take of the Chalice and Bread.

V.

Ay, pray on thy knees, that each old rural fane
    They have left to the bat and the mole,
May sound with the loud-pealing organ again,
    And the full-swelling voice of the soul.
Peradventure, when next thou shalt journey thereby,
    Even-bells shall ring out on the air,
And the dim-lighted windows reveal to thine eye
    The snowy-robed pastor at prayer.

Chelsea.

I.

WHEN old Canúte the Dane
  Was merry England's king;
  A thousand years agone, and more,
  As ancient rymours sing;
  His boat was rowing down the Ouse,
At eve, one summer day,
Where Ely's tall cathedral peered
Above the glassy way.

II.

Anon, sweet music on his ear,
  Comes floating from the fane,
And listening, as with all his soul,
  Sat old Canúte the Dane;

And reverent did he doff his crown,
    To join the clerkly prayer,
While swelled old lauds and litanies
    Upon the stilly air.

III.

Now, who shall glide on Hudson's breast,
    At eve of summer day,
And cometh where St. Peter's tower
    Peers o'er his coasting way: .
A moment, let him slack his oar,
    And speed more still along,
His ears shall catch those very notes
    Of litany and song.

IV.

The Church that sung those anthem prayers
    A thousand years ago,
Is singing yet by silver Cam,
    And here by Hudson's flow:
And GLORIAS that thrilled the heart
    Of old Canúte the Dane,
Are rising yet, at morn and eve,
    From Chelsea's student train.

V.

VENITE EXULTEMUS, there,
  Those ancient scholars sung,
And JUBILATE DOMINO
  The vaulted alleys rung:
And our gray pile with tremble oft
  Beneath the organ's roar,
When here those very matin-songs
  With high TE DEUM pour.

VI.

And where are kings and empires now,
  Since then, that went and came?
But holy Church is praying yet,
  A thousand years the same!
And these that sing shall pass away;
  New choirs their room shall fill:
Be sure thy children's children here
  Shall hear those anthems still.

VII.

For not like kingdoms of the world
  The holy Church of GOD!
Though earthquake-shocks be rocking it,
  And tempest is abroad;

Unshaken as eternal hills,
    Unmovable it stands,
A mountain that shall fill the earth,
    A fane unbuilt by hands.

VIII.

Though years fling ivy over it,
    Its cross peers high in air,
And reverend with majestic age,
    Eternal youth is there!
Oh mark her holy battlements,
    And her foundations strong;
And hear, within, her ceaseless voice,
    And her unending song!

IX.

Oh ye, that in these latter days
    The citadel defend,
Perchance for you, the Saviour said
    I'm with you—to the end:
Stand therefore girt about, and hold
    Your burning lamps in hand,
And standing, listen for your LORD,
    And till He cometh—stand!

x.

The gates of hell shall ne'er prevail
  Against our holy home,
But oh be wakeful sentinels,
  Until the Master come!
The night is spent—but listen ye;
  For on its deepest calm,
What marvel if the cry be heard,
  The marriage of the Lamb!

Vigils.

Let your loins be girded about, and your lights burning:
And ye yourselves like unto men that wait for their lord, when he will return from the wedding;
Blessed are those servants whom the Lord, when He cometh, shall find watching:
And if He shall come in the second watch, or come in the third watch, and find them so, blessed are those servants.—*The Holy Gospel in the Ordering of Deacons.*

I.

'T is the fall of eve;
And the long tapers, now, we light
And watch: for we believe
Our LORD may come at night.
     Adeste Fideles.

II

An hour—and it is SEVEN,
And fast away the evening rolls:
   Oh it is dark in heaven,
But light within our souls.
         Veni Creator SPIRITUS!

III.

Hark! the old bell strikes EIGHT!
And still we watch with heart and ear,
   For as the hour grows late
The Day-star may be near.
         Jubilate DEO!

IV.

Hark! it is knelling NINE!
But faithful eyes grow never dim;
   And still our tapers shine,
And still ascends our hymn.
         Cum Angelis!

The watchman crieth TEN!
My soul, be watching for the Light,
   For when He comes agen,
'Tis—as the thief at night.
         Nisi Dominus!

VI.

By the old bell—ELEVEN !
Now trim thy lamp, and ready stand;
The world to sleep is given,
But JESUS is at hand.
   Kyrie Eleison !

VII.

At MIDNIGHT—is a cry !
Is it the bridegroom draweth near?
Come quickly, LORD, for I
Have longed Thy voice to hear !
   De profundis !

VIII.

Could ye not watch ONE hour?
Be ready: or the bridal train
 And Bridegroom, with His dower,
May sweep along in vain.
   Miserere mei !

IX.

By the old steeple—Two !
And now I know the day is near !

Watch—for His word is true,
And JESUS may appear!
   Dies Iræ.

X.

Three—by the drowsy chime!
And joy is nearer than at first.
 Oh, let us watch the time
When the first light shall burst!
   Sursum corda!

XI.

Four—and a streak of day!
At the cock-crowing He may come;
 And still to all I say,
Watch—and with awe be dumb.
   Fili David!

XII.

Five!—and the tapers now
In rosy morning dimly burn!
 Stand, and be girded thou;
Thy LORD will yet return!
   Veni JESU!

XIII.

Hark! 'tis the Matin-call!
Oh, when our Lord shall come agen,
At prime or even fall,
Blest are the wakeful men!
Nunc dimittis.

Matin Bells.

I myself will awake right early.—Psalter.

I.

THE Sun is up betimes,
 And the dappled East is blushing,
And the merry matin-chimes,
 They are gushing—Christian—gushing!
They are tolling in the tower,
 For another day begun;
And to hail the rising hour
 Of a brighter, brighter Sun.

Rise—Christian—rise!
  For a sunshine brighter far
Is breaking o'er thine eyes,
  Than the bonny morning star!

II.

The lark is in the sky,
  And his morning-note is pouring:
He hath a wing to fly,
  So he's soaring—Christian—soaring!
His nest is on the ground,
  But only in the night;
For he loves the matin-sound,
  And the highest heaven's height.
Hark—Christian—hark!
  At heaven-door he sings!
And be thou like the lark,
  With thy soaring spirit-wings!

III.

The merry matin-bells,
  In their watch-tower they are swinging;
For the day is o'er the dells,
  And they're singing—Christian—singing!
They have caught the morning beam
  Through their ivied turret's wreath,

And the chancel-window's gleam
   Is glorious beneath:
Go—Christian—go,
   For the altar flameth there,
And the snowy vestments glow,
   Of the presbyter at prayer!

IV.

There is morning incense flung
   From the child-like lily-flowers;
And their fragrant censer swung,
   Make it ours—Christian—ours!
And hark, our Mother's hymn,
   And the organ-peals we love!
They sound like cherubim
   At their orisons above!
Pray—Christian—pray
   At the bonny peep of dawn,
Ere the dew-drop and the spray
   That christen it, are gone!

The Curfew

I.

N each New-England village,
    At nine o'clock at night,
Still rings old England's curfew,
    And says—put out the light!
Then tell they to their children,
    Of long long years ago,
The tale of Battle-Abbey,
    How they fought with shaft and bow.

II.

But here's another story
    New-England wives may tell,
How he that bade the curfew
    Heard an unbidden bell;
And let the boy that listens
    Which best he liketh say,

The bell that rings for darkness,
  Or the bell that rings for day.

III.

When William lay a-dying,
  All dull of eye and dim,
And he that conquered Harold
  Felt One that conquered him;
He recked not of the minutes,
  The midnight, or the morn,
But there he lay—unbreathing
  As the babe that is still-born.

IV.

But suddenly a bell tolled!
  He started from the swound,
First glared, and then grew gentle,
  Then wildly stared around.
He deemed 'twas bell at even,
  To quench the Saxon's coal,
But oh, it was a curfew
  To quench his fiery soul.

V.

Now, prithee, holy father!
  What means this bell, I pray?

Is't curfew-time in England,
    Or am I far away?
GOD wot—it moves my spirit,
    As if it ev'n might be
The bells of mine own city,
    In dear old Normandie.

VI.

Ay, sire—thou art in Rouen;
    And 'tis the prayer-bell's chime
In the steeple of St. Mary's,
    That tolls the hour of prime!
Then bid them pray for William,
    And may the Virgin-born,
In the church of His sweet mother,
    Hear their praying, this blest morn.

VII.

Little dream the kneeling people
    Who joins them in their prayers!
They deem not stout King William
    Their paternoster shares:
Nor see they how he lifteth
    With theirs, his dying hand—
The hand that, from the Saxon,
    Tore the crown of fair England:

VIII.

Nor heard they—as responding
  To their chaunting oft he sighed,
Till rose their DE PROFUNDIS,
  And the mighty Norman died.
And I have thought, who knoweth,
  But if that early toll,
Like the contrite malefactor's,
  Moved a dying sinner's soul!

IX.

And we, the Seed of England,
  Hear yet the curfew's knell;
Oh might we learn from William
  That soul-awaking bell!
Then should the sound that covers
  At night the cheery coal,
Stir, too, the morning-embers
  Of worship in the soul.

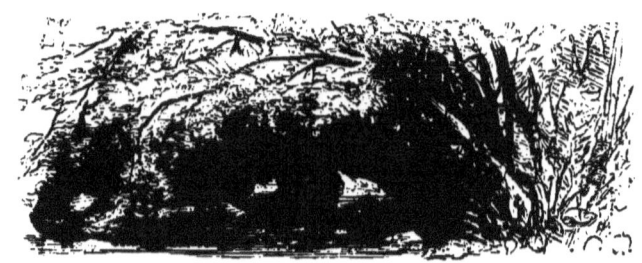

Wildminster.

An altar of earth thou shalt make unto Me.—*Exodus.*

I.

O where the mossy rock shall be
    Thy nature-hallowed shrine,
The leafy copse thy canopy,
    Its fringe, the gadding vine!
There let the clusters round that blush,
    Be sacramental Blood,
And fountains, by the feet that gush,
    Thy pure baptizing flood.

II.

There let the snowy lawn be spread
    Upon the turfy mound:
There break the life-bestowing Bread,
    And bless the people round.

There, the green bush thy chancel-rail,
    Its cushion'd floor the sod,
Bid welcome, to the silvan pale,
    The kneeling host of GOD.

III.

Look up, and fretted vaults are there,
    And heaven itself shines through,
Or evening is depictured fair,
    The starlight, and the blue!
A temple never built by hands,
    And many a shadowed aisle,
There—where the columned forest stands,
    Be thy cathedral pile!

IV.

There, are full choir and antiphon
    At lauds and vesper-time,
And every niche rings unison
    With priestly voice, at prime:
There, shall thy solitary soul
    Find out its cloister dim,
With not the labouring organ's roll,
    But nature's gushing hymn.

V.

There, the full flowers their odours fling
    To bid thee pour thy prayer,
And vines their fragrant censers swing
    O'er all the hallowed air.
Thy heart forth-flaming to the skies
    Shall like their breath be given,
And like consuming incense rise
    In sweetness up to heaven.

VI.

Go to the harvest-whitened West,
    Ye surpliced priests of GOD,
In all the Christian armour drest,
    And with the Gospel shod:
Go, for their feet are beautiful
    That on the mountain stand,
And, more than music, musical,
    The watchman's voice at hand.

VII.

Go, for the midnight wanes apace;
    The Sun himself is nigh!
Go to the wild and lonely place,
    And in the desert cry.

Go,—and the greenwoods are thy fanes,
    Thine altars—every sod:
Say to the wilderness, He reigns,
    Thy Saviour and thy GOD!

VIII.

Lo! where the unsent heralds run,
    Why wait Thy priests, oh LORD!
These that were bid, from sun to sun,
    To preach the Gospel word?
Oh to Thine harvest, Saviour, send
    The hosts of Thine employ,
To reap the ripened sheaves that bend,
    And shout them home with joy!

Nashotah.

AMERICAN MISSIONS.

I.

H Lord, our Lord, how spreads that little seed
Which was, at first, of every seed the least!
The birds of air shall scarce its growth outspeed:
Its world-wide branches knit the West and East.

II.

But how it makes my heart of hearts upswell
    To see our English ritual planted there,
Where walks his round Nashotah's sentinel,
    And breaks its daily service on the air!

III.

Rude as the Saviour's birthplace are its halls,
    O'er which, like Bethlehem's star, the cross appears:
And oft the watchman of those outpost walls
    In tented fields his wakeful voice uprears.

IV.

Oft, on their summer-mission, as they fare,
    They seek the wildwood settler's far retreat,
And rear their curtained chapel—while, to prayer,
    The forest-dwellers haste with ready feet.

V.

And where, at dawn, the prairie-fox did bark,
    Are heard, by night, sweet canticle and chaunt:
Where sung before no choirist but the lark,
    Ring out the Church's anthems jubilant!

VI.

Then, in the wilderness, is heard the voice
    Of one that, like the Baptist, bids repent;
While the rude trappers tremblingly rejoice,
    And hearts, long-hardened, soften and relent.

VII.

And there the Norway rover, or the Swede,
    Kneels with frank Switzer, and the florid Dane;
And England's exile weeps to find the seed
    His mother scattered—bound in sheaves again:

VIII.

While here and there, those mingled groups amid,
    The smoking torches shew the desert-child;
The sad Oneida's countenance, half hid,
    The bloody Osage—tamed, yet darkly wild.

IX.

Flares on the Negro's swarth the self-same blaze:
    Nor lacks the scene, from Shem's sad tents, some one;
Nashotah's priests have found, in desert ways,
    Rebecca's child and Isaac's homeless son.

X.

Thus, in the outskirt earth, earth's races meet,
    For such their Maker's wonderful award,
And, at our Mother's fair unfetter'd feet,
    Learn of the Cross, and bow to own its LORD!

XI.

Another service greets the morrow's dawn,
    And babes are christened, and a prayer-book left:
Then—in a trice—priest, chapel, all are gone:
    'Tis something if the woodman feels bereft!

XII.

Oh might our Mother's caitiff sons that rend
    Her yearning bowels, in the mother-land,
See how she blesses thus the far world's end,
    And lift for pardoning grace their guilty hand!

XIII.

Hear, then, my plaint, ye white-robed youth that raise
    By stately Cam the even or morning song,
And when in turn ye wear the Senate's bays,
    Avenge—your fathers' shame—our Mother's wrong.

XIV.

And you, ye clerks, 'neath Oxford's glorious domes
    That kneel, full oft, too listless at your prayers.
Think of the rites that bless these forest homes,
    And yours, perchance, shall be as blest as theirs.

XV.

For not your hymns that Wykeham's roofs rebound,
    Not Waynflete's arches wake such deep delight,
As that Nashotah's wilds alike resound
    The self-same prayers, and own the same sweet rite!

XVI.

Oh 'tis the glory of our service blest
    Not that alone cathedrals hear it sung,
But that its music cheers the world's wild West,
    And swells in rudeness from the woodman's tongue

XVII.

And oft I think—what joy and strength, in GOD,
    Prophetic vision of what thus I sing,
Had given to saintly Ken, or martyred Laud,
    When seemed the Church half dead with suffering!

XVIII.

Or even to him, the frail but reverend sire,
 Whose palsied palm passed down the lineal grace,
Yes—even to Cranmer, with that palm on fire,
 And Moses' radiance on his dying face;

XIX.

Had he the Australian wilderness foreseen,
 Canadian fastness, and the torrid land,
And priests, despising seas that roll between,
 By CHRIST commissioned, through his flaming hand!

XX.

Rejoice we, then, remembering other times
 When hung the Church's life upon a thread,
That GOD hath slain her tyrants for their crimes,
 And raised her up, immortal, from the dead!

St. Silvan's Bell.

Desire of me, and I shall give thee the heathen for thine inheritance, and the utmost parts of the earth for thy possession.—*Psalter.*

I.

A FORTNIGHT it was from Whitsuntide,
    And a service was said that day,
In a little church, that a good man built
    In the wilderness far away.
A twelve-month before, and there was not there
    Or temple or holy bell;
But the place it was free from holiness
    As the soul of the Infidel.

II.

Five thousand years this world is old,
    And twice four hundred more,

And that green spot had forest been
  From the eldest days of yore:
And there had the red-man made his hut,
  And the savage beast his lair,
But never, since this old earth was young,
  Was it hallowed with Christian prayer.

III.

But now, for the first, a bell rung out,
  Through the aisles of the wild greenwood,
And echo came back from the far far trees,
  Like the holla of Robin Hood:
And the red-deer woke, in his bosky nook,
  That strange strange sound to hear,
And the jessamine-buds from his side he shook,
  And he listened awhile in fear.

IV.

But the bell that rings for the Prince of Peace
  Is never a beast's alarm,
And down went his antlered head agen,
  Like an infant asleep on its arm:
And the woodman went by, and stirred him not,
  With his wife and children round,
And the baby leaped up on its mother's breast,
  And laughed at the church-bell's sound.

V.

For the babe, he was all unchristened yet,
  And well might he leap for joy;
A fountain was gushing, where rung that bell,
  That should make him a Christian boy.
And his mother—she thought of the Catechist,
  And she blessed the LORD above,
That her child should be baptized for CHRIST,
  And taught in His fear and love.

VI.

And she prayed in her heart, as Hannah prayed,
  He might kneel in the chancel fair,
Like children they brought to the LORD of old,
  To be blest with the bishop's prayer:
And she saw, far off, the vested priest,
  The ring, and the marriage-bann,
Making some maiden a happy wife,
  And her boy a happier man.

VII.

And the bell rung on; and the wood sent forth,
  From their log-built homes around,
The yeomanry all with their families
  A-wondering at the sound:

And tears I saw in an old man's eye,
    That came from a far countree;
It minded his inmost soul, he said,
    Of the church-bells over the sea.

VIII.

For a boy was he, in England, once,
    And he loved the merry chimes;
Had heard them ring out of a Whitsuntide,
    And waken the holiday-times!
And a boy was he when hither he came,
    But now he was old and gray;
He had not thought that a Christian bell
    Should toll on his burial-day.

IX.

A boy was he when he first swung axe
    Against the strong oak limb;
He was gray-haired now, when he heard the bell
    And threw it away from him;
And he followed the sound—for he thought of home,
    And the motherly hand so fair,
That led him along through the churchyard mounds,
    And made him kneel down to prayer.

X.

And now did an organ's peal break out,
    And the bell-notes died away:
And a holy bishop, in robes, was there,
    And priests in their white array.
And I heard a voice go up the nave,
    And the priests, responding plain;
Lift up your heads, ye gates—they said,
    For the King of Glory's train!

XI.

And I could not but weep, for I knew, on high,
    The Saviour had asked of GOD,
That the utmost lands might all be His,
    And the ground whereon I trod;
And I blessed the good LORD, that here at length
    His own true heralds came,
To challenge for CHRIST His heritage,
    And hallow it with His Name.

XII.

Now pray with me, that ever there
    St. Silvan's bell may ring,
And the yeoman brave, with their children all,
    The praise of the Saviour sing:

And pray ye still, that, further west,
    The song of the bell may sound,
Till the land, from sea to sea, is blest,
    And the world is holy ground.

Daily Service.

One day telleth another.—Psalter.

I.

WHEN the gorgeous day begins
    In the world's remotest East,
And the sun his pathway wins,
    Bringing back some glorious feast:
There, forestalling fears and sins,
Kneels the faithful English priest:
There the altar glitters fair,
Spread for Eucharistic prayer.

II.

And as each meridian line,
    Gains the travelled sun, that day,

Still begin those rites divine,
  Still new priests begin to pray;
Still are blest the bread and wine,
  Still one prayer salutes his ray :
Continent and ocean round
Rolls the tided wave of sound!

III.

Then at last the prairied West
  Sees the festal light appear,
And Nashotah's clerks, from rest,
  Early rise, their song to rear;
Gird they then the snowy vest,
  Raise they then the anthem clear;
Anthems in the East that rose,
Girded earth—and there must close.

IV.

But when, there, the holy light
  Fades adown their west afar,
And begins the vesper rite,
  Faithful as the vesper star,
Then—just then—has passed the night,
  Where our eastern altars are;
And another daylight fair
Wakes a new earth-girding prayer.

V.

Brethren of the West—my soul
   Oft, to you, will westward wing,
When some hymn ascendeth whole
   At the hour of offering,
Thinking how 'twill onward roll
   Till your voice the same shall sing;
Uttered o'er and o'er agen,
Till ye give the last Amen.

VI.

That same hymn, ere I have sung,
   Hath been sung in England's fanes,
And perchance, in barbarous tongue,
   'Mid the Orient hills and plains;
And—to die the woods among,
   Swells, from aisles and tinted panes,
To the forest's solemn cells,
Where the roving red-man dwells.

VII.

Moves my spirit at the thought
   That our service, Anglican,
From the faithful Isle, hath caught
   Thus. the many hearts of man;

For this sign our GOD hath wrought,
   'Gainst the heartless Roman's ban ;
Seal of life, and fire divine,
Mother, in those words of Thine!

VIII.

One—in water sanctified,
   Though the claim be long forgot ;
One—in blood from JESU's side,
   Though proud Trent confess it not ;
One—in Spirit, far and wide,
   With each ancient part and lot ;
Mother, let me ever be
One with CHRIST and one with Thee!

Christmas Carol.

I.

CAROL, carol, Christians,
　　Carol joyfully;
Carol for the coming
　　Of Christ's Nativity;
And pray a gladsome Christmas
For all good Christian men;

CHRISTMAS CAROL.

Carol, carol, Christians,
  For Christmas, come agen.
      Carol, carol.

II.

Go ye to the forest,
  Where the myrtles grow,
Where the pine and laurel
  Bend beneath the snow:
Gather them for JESUS;
  Wreathe them for His shrine;
Make His temple glorious
  With the box and pine.
      Carol, carol.

III.

Wreath your Christmas garland,
  Where to CHRIST we pray:
It shall smell like Carmel
  On our festal day;
Libanus and Sharon
  Shall not greener be
Than our holy chancel
  On CHRIST's Nativity.
      Carol, carol.

IV.

Carol, carol, Christians!
  Like the Magi now,
Ye must lade your caskets
  With a grateful vow:
Ye must have sweet incense,
  Myrrh, and finest gold,
At our Christmas altar
  Humbly to unfold.
          Carol, carol.

V.

Blow, blow up the trumpet,
  For our solemn feast,
Gird thine armour, Christian,
  Wear thy surplice, priest!
Go ye to the altar,
  Pray, with fervour pray,
For JESUS' second coming,
  And the Latter Day.
          Carol, carol.

VI.

Give us grace, oh Saviour,
  To put off in might,

Deeds and dreams of darkness,
    For the robes of light!
And to live as lowly,
    As Thyself with men;
So to rise in glory,
    When Thou com'st agen.
            Carol, carol.

Christening.

I.

H, if there be a sight, on earth,
    That makes good angels smile,
'Tis when a soul of mortal birth
    Is washed from mortal guile:

II.

When some repentant child of Eve's,
    In age, is born anew:
Or when, on life's first buds and leaves,
    Falls the baptismal dew.

III.

But all the same! The soul that, in
    That laver undefiled,

Is truly washed from wrath and sin,
    Must be a little child.

IV.

Children alone that grace may claim,
    Whether, to babes, be given,
Or to the childlike heart, the name
    Of all the sons of Heaven!

V.

See, then, the font, the church's door,
    The group with gladsome look,
The waters, and the priest to pour,
    The sponsors, and the book!

VI.

What light is on all faces, now,
    As low they bend to pray!
How kindly on the grandsire's brow
    Each furrow smooths away!

VII.

How fond the pale young mother's eye
    Lights up, with tearful charm,
To see her babe enfolded lie
    Upon the surpliced arm!

VIII.

And he, of innocence, that wears
    That sign and spotless vest,
How Shepherd-like! Like Him that bears
    The lambkin on His breast.

IX.

But hark! the tiny Christian's name!
    Hush! 'Tis the Mystic Trine!
The Water and the SPIRIT came,
    And, there, is life divine.

X.

The Cross is signed—mysterious seal
    Of death our life that won:
And CHRIST's dear spouse, for woe or weal,
    Hath borne her Lord a son.

XI.

For woe or weal! The grafted shoot,
    Alas! may fade and die;
Though long the fatness of the Root
    This shower of grace supply.

XII.

But, JESU! take Thy child from earth
  Ere sense and guile begin,
If, only so, this second birth
  May 'scape the death of sin.

The Calendar.

I.

Y Prayer-book is a casket bright,
　　With gold and incense stored,
Which, every day, and every night,
　　I open to the LORD:
Yet when I first unclasp its lids,
　　I find a bunch of myrrh
Embalming all our mortal life;
　　The Church's Calendar.

II.

But who would see an almanac
　　When opes his Book of Prayer?
Of all the leaves between its lids,
　　These, only, are not fair!

So said I, in my thoughtless years,
    But now, with awe, I scan
The Calendar, like Sybil-leaves
    That tell the life of Man.

III.

God set the sun and moon for signs:
    The Church His signs doth know,
And here—while sleeps the sluggish world,
    She marks them as they go.
Here for His coming looks she forth
    As, for her spouse, the bride;
Here, at her lattice, faithfully
    She waits the morning-tide.

IV.

All time is hers, and, at its end,
    Her Lord shall come with more:
As one for whom all time was made,
    Thus guardeth she her store;
And, doating o'er her letters old,
    As pores the wife bereft,
Thus daily reads the Bride of Christ
    Each message He hath left.

V.

As prisoners notch their tally-stick,
    And wait the far-off day,
So marks she days, and months, and years,
    To ponder and to pray;
And year by year beginning new
    Her faithful task sublime,
How lovingly she meteth out
    Each portion in its time!

VI.

This little index of thy life,
    Thou, all thy life, shalt find
So teaching thee to tell thy days,
    That wisdom thou may'st mind.
Oh live thou by the Calendar;
    And, when each morn you kneel,
Note how the numbered days go by,
    Like spokes in Time's swift wheel.

VII.

With this thy closet seek; and learn
    What strengthening word, to-day,
From out the Holy Book of God
    Our Mother would display;

And know thy prayers go up on high,
  With thousands that, unknown,
Are lighted at the self-same fire,
  And mingle at God's throne.

VIII.

For so—though severed far on earth—
  Together we are fed ;
And onward, though we see it not,
  Together we are sped !
Oh live ye by the Calendar,
  And with the good ye dwell ;
The Spirit that comes down on them
  Shall lighten you as well.

The Soul-Dirge.

Then said Jesus, Will ye also go away?—St. John.

I.

THE organ played sweet music
    Whileas, on Easter-day,
All heartless from the altar,
    The heedless went away:
    And down the broad aisle crowding,
They seemed a funeral train,
That were burying their spirits
    To the music of that strain.

II.

As I listened to the organ,
    And saw them crowd along,

I thought I heard two voices,
    Speaking strangely, but not strong ;
And one, it whispered sadly,
    Will ye also go away?
But the other spoke exulting,
    Ha! the soul-dirge,—hear it play!

III.

Hear the soul-dirge! hear the soul-dirge!
    And see the feast divine!
Ha! the jewels of salvation,
    And the trampling feet of swine!
Hear the soul-dirge! hear the soul-dirge!
    Little think they, as they go,
What priceless pearls they tread on,
    Who spurn their SAVIOUR so!

IV.

Hear the soul-dirge! hear the soul-dirge!
    It was dread to hear it play,
While the famishing went crowding
    From the Bread of Life away:
They were bidden, they were bidden
    To their Father's festal board ;
But they all, with gleeful faces,
    Turned their back upon the LORD.

V.

You had thought the church a prison,
    Had you seen how they did pour,
With giddy, giddy faces,
    From the consecrated door.
There was angels' food all ready,
    But the bidden—where were they?
O'er the highways and the hedges,
    Ere the soul-dirge cease to play!

VI.

Oh, the soul-dirge, how it echoed
    The emptied aisles along,
As the open street grew crowded
    With the full outpouring throng!
And then—again the voices;
    Ha! the soul-dirge! hear it play!
And the pensive, pensive whisper,
    Will ye also go away?

VII.

Few, few were they that lingered
    To sup with JESUS there;
And yet, for all that spurned Him,
    There was plenty, and to spare!

And now, the food of angels
    Uncovered to my sight,
All-glorious was the altar,
    And the chalice glittered bright.

VIII.

Then came the hymn TRISAGION,
    And rapt me up on high,
With angels and archangels
    To laud and magnify.
I seemed to feast in Heaven;
    And downward wafted then,
With angels chaunting róund me,
    Good-will and peace to men.

IX.

I may not tell the rapture
    Of a banquet so divine;
Ho! every one that thirsteth,
    Let him taste the bread and wine
Hear the Bride and Spirit, saying
    Will ye also go away?
Or—go, poor soul, forever!
    Oh! the soul-dirge—hear it play!

The Church's Daughter.

I.

O H woman is a tender tree!
    The hand must gentle be that rears
Through storm and sunshine, patiently,
    That plant of grace, of smiles and tears.

II.

Let her that waters, at the font,
    Life's earliest blossoms, have the care;
And where the garden's LORD is wont
    To walk His round—oh keep her there.

III.

Who but her Mother Church, knows well
    The deep-hid springs of grief and joy,
That in the heart of woman swell,
    And make that heart—or else destroy!

IV.

Who but the Church, can every power
    Of the true woman nurse to life,
Till, fit for every changeful hour,
    Is seen the maiden—woman—wife!

V.

'Tis not alone the radiant face,
    And some accomplished gifts, that shine;
The harmony of every grace
    Is nurtured by her care divine.

VI.

She—not the coy and bashful art,
    But all the instinct of the pure,
The virgin soul—the angel heart,
    Alone is mindful to mature.

VII.

Even like the first warm sun of May,
    Or, to the daisy, April showers,
Her earliest lesson—how to pray,
    Clothes the young soul with fragrant flowers.

VIII.

Then, planted by the altar's pale,
    The Church, with catechising art,
Trains to the chancel's trellised rail
    The wandering tendrils of the heart.

IX.

And when before the mitred priest
    She bids, at length, her daughter kneel,
What lavish gifts of grace increased
    Shine from her dear Redeemer's seal!

X.

Or when, her snowy veil beneath,
    She stands a pale and fearful thing,
And, trembling like her orange-wreath,
    Gives her fair finger to the ring;

XI.

When manly honour makes her bride,
   In God's own name, Triune and dread,
And, from the holy altar's side,
   Another blessing crowns her head;

XII.

See how the Church's care, for her,
   Hath done the jealous parent's part,
And been to him a monitor
   To whom she gives her daughter's heart!

XIII.

Nor shall she e'er desert, through life,
   Through fearful life, that daughter's side,
But ever, o'er the wedded wife,
   Bend fond, as o'er the kneeling bride.

XIV.

When the pale mother clasps her child,
   And pats her darling to its rest,
Or sinks to slumbers undefiled,
   Her bride-ring shining o'er her breast;

XV.

Again, to hollow that pure joy,
   Comes Holy Church and tells her, then,
Of Mary and the Holy Boy,
   And claims the turtle-doves agen.

XVI.

Or if, within the darken'd room,
   The trail of death be sweeping slow,
The Church that taught her unto Whom,
   Shall teach her, too, the way to go.

XVII.

Then spreads she, there, an altar lone;
   Her priest, to bless and break, is there,
And angels, radiant from the throne,
   Come winging round the scene of prayer.

XVIII.

So points the Church to Paradise,
   And bids, in peace, her child depart;
Then shuts to earth the blessed eyes,
   And binds with balm each bleeding heart.

XIX.

Then roses pale, and rose-marine,
    She scatters o'er the marble dust;
And at the last heart-rending scene,
    As earth takes back its precious trust;

XX.

From the deep grave she lifts the eye,
    Where the free spirit wings hath found;
And leaves her child's mortality,
    To rise an angel from the ground.

I Love the Church.

I

I LOVE the Church,—the holy Church,
　　The Saviour's spotless bride;
And oh, I love her palaces
　　Through all the land so wide:
The cross-topped spire amid the trees,
　　The holy bell of prayer;
The music of our Mother's voice,
　　Our Mother's home is there!

II.

The village tower—'tis joy to me;
　　I cry the LORD is here!
The village bells—they fill my soul;
　　They more than fill mine ear!

O'er kingdoms to the Saviour won,
    Their triumph-peal is hurled;
Their sound is now in all the earth,
    Their words throughout the world.

III.

And here—eternal ocean cross'd,
    And long, long ages past,
In climes beyond the setting sun,
    They preach the LORD at last;
And here, Redeemer, are Thy priests
    Unbroken in array,
Far from Thine Holy Sepulchre,
    And Thine Ascension day!

IV.

Unbroken in their lineage,
    Their warrants clear as when
Thou, Saviour, didst go up on high,
    And give good gifts to men;
Here, clothed in innocence they stand,
    To shed Thy mercy wide,
Baptizing to the Trinal Name,
    With waters from Thy side.

V.

And here, confessors of Thy cross,
    Thine holy orders three,
The bishop, and the elders too,
    And lowly deacons be;
To rule and feed the flock of CHRIST,
    To fight, of faith, the strife,
And to the host of GOD's Elect,
    To break the Bread of Life.

VI.

Here rises, with the rising morn,
    Their incense unto Thee,
Their bold confession Catholic,
    And high doxology:
Soul-melting litany is here,
    And here—each holy feast,
Up to the altar, duly spread,
    Ascends the stoled priest.

VII.

Then with the message of our King,
    The herald stands on high:
How beautiful the feet of them
    That on the mountain cry!

And then—as when the doors were shut,
    With JESUS left alone,
The faithful sup with CHRIST—and He
    In breaking bread is known.

VIII.

And kneeling at the altar's rail,
    With blessings all divine,
As from the Saviour's hand, they take
    The broken bread, and wine;
In one communion with the saints,
    With angels and the blest,
And looking for the blessed hope
    Of an eternal rest.

IX.

The peace of GOD is on their heads;
    And so they wend away,
To homes all cheerful with the light
    Of love's inspiring ray:
And through the churchyard and the graves,
    With kindly tears they fare,
Where every turf was decent laid,
    And hallowed by a prayer.

X.

The dead in CHRIST—they rest in hope;
  And o'er their sleep sublime,
The shadow of the steeple moves,
  From morn to vesper-chime:
On every mound, in solemn shade,
  Its imaged cross doth lie,
As goes the sunlight to the West
  Or rides the moon on high.

XI.

I love the Church—the holy Church,
  That o'er our life presides,
The birth, the bridal, and the grave,
  And many an hour besides!
Be mine, through life, to live in her,
  And, when the LORD shall call,
To die in her—the spouse of CHRIST,
  The Mother of us all.

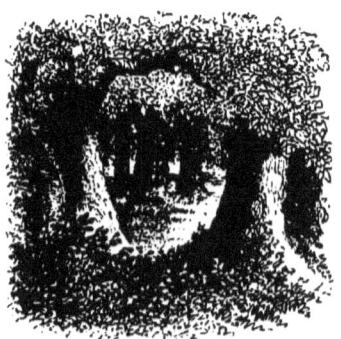

ITALIAN VERSIONS.

BY COUNT TASCA.

IO AMO LA CHIESA.

I.

AMO la Chiesa! Ah! sì la Chiesa santa,
Del Salvator l' immacolata sposa:
Amo i sacri edifizj onde s' ammanta
Dell' Anglia la contrada spaziosa;
La croce del pignon fra pianta e pianta
Della prece la squilla armoniosa;
Della voce materna il suon diletto
Che nostra Madre è là sotto quel tetto.

II.

E del villaggio il campanile, oh! quanto
Piacer mi desta! Io sclamo; è qui 'l Signore!
Delle campane il suon che aggrado tanto
Più che gli orecchi mi riempie il core.
Il trionfal lor grido ovunque è spanto
Pei regni che sommise il Salvatore,
Diffuso è in terra il lor squillo giocondo
Ed il linguaggio lor per tutto il mondo.

III.

Qui dopo il volger di ben lunga etade,
  Dell' immenso oceano oltre il confine
  Ed oltre le spiaggie ove il sol cade,
  Esse il Signor han proclamato alfine.
Qui son tuoi preti, o Cristo, in lor pietade
  Fidi alle pure antiche discipline,
  Lunge dal santo avello u' l' uman velo
  Posasti, e d' ond' Tu salisti al cielo.

IV.

L' ordin di succession non mai troncato,
  Legale è il lor poter, come il tuo l' era
  Quando salendo al cielo hai ricolmato
  D' ogni tuo ben l' umanitade intera.
Qui ciascun d'essi d'innocenza ornato
  Lunge diffonde la tua grazia vera,
  E battezzando va nel nome Trino
  Coll' acque uscite dal tuo sen divino.

V.

E qui della Tua croce confessori
  Stan tuoi ministri in triplo ordine espressi:
  I vescovi da prima ed i seniori,
  Quind' ad entrambi i diaconi sommessi,
Son del gregge cristian guide e pastori:
  Per la Fe' combattendo obblian se stessi,
  Ed ai convivi che il Signore invita
  Rompendo vanno il pane della vita.

VI.

Pria che dei monti sol dori le cime,
Col cattolico e fermo atto di fede
E colla lor dossologia sublime,
Qui sal l' incenso del tuo trono al piede,
E litania che dolce in cor s' imprime ;
E ad ogni santa a noi festa che riede
All' altar che, qual deesi, ornato splende
Cinto di stola il sacerdote ascende.

VII.

Poi del Re nostro fia che il nunzio apporte
Dall' alto seggio la parola eletta.
Oh ! quanto è bello il progredir del forte
Che sale a predicar del monte in vetta !
Poi, come allor che si sevrar' le porte,
Gesù lasciato sol, la prediletta
Cena fedel con Cristo, ov' Egli poi
Rompendo il pane si rivela a noi.

VIII.

Ed umilmente inginocchiati presso
   L' altar, col don d' ogni favor divino,
   Qual dalla man del Salvator istesso,
   Prendono il pan ridotto in pezzi e 'l vino,
In comunion coi santi e nell' amplesso
   D' ogni beato e d' ogni serafino :
Assorti nel desio che il dì superno
Per lor riluca del riposo eterno.

IX.

Colla pace di Dio sul volto e in seno
  Fan poi dal tempio al tetto lor passaggio,
Tutt' esultanti in quel lume sereno
  Che d' amor ne' lor petti infonde un raggio.
Lungo il sacrato che di tombe è pieno
  Offron di pianto ai morti un dolce omaggio;
Là consacrate dal pregar, di molle
Erba e di fior s' ammantano le zolle;

X.

I morti in Cristo dormono sperando,
  E coprendo il lor sonno alto e tranquillo
L' ombra del campanil gira da quando
  Il sole spunta al vespertino squillo:
Ogni zolla in solenne ombra mostrando
  Vien della croce l'immortal vessillo,
O l' maggior astro all' occidente scenda,
O la pallida luna in ciel risplenda.

XI.

Amo la Chiesa, ah! sì la Chiesa santa
  Che la nostra quaggiù vita presiede, ·
E culla, e nozze, e funerali, e quanta
  Altra serie d' eventi a noi succede.
Ah! ch' io sempre in lei viva! E quando infranta
  Mia vita, assunto alla tremenda sede
Del giudizio sarò, ch' io muoja in lei . . .
  Tu sposa a CRISTO e Madre nostra sei!

IL SERVIZIO DIVINO.

"UN GIORNO CHIAMA L'ALTRO,"—Salmo, 19.

I.

QUANDO l' oriental lido remoto
  Manda del dì la prima e vaga luce,
  E 'l sol poggiando per l' etereo vuoto
  Qualche festa solenne riconduce,
  Timori e colpe a prevenir, devoto
  L' anglo-prete ad orar là si conduce:
  Per la cena eucaristica parato
  Risplendente è l' altar più dell' usato.

II.

Ad ogni ora che il sole in suo cammino
  Marca sul meridiano in simil giorno
  Ricomincia il fedel rito divino;
  Nuovi preti al pregar fanno ritorno
  Benedicendo sempre il pane e 'l vino:
  Nuova preghiera il sol saluta, e intorno
  Sul continente e sovra il mar, pertutto
  Del suon si spande il progredente flutto.

III.

Poi d' Occidente le savane il santo
  Lume vedere alla lor volta ponno:
  E pronti i chierci di Nashota intanto
  Per unirsi a cantar rompon lor sonno:

Cinti di bianchi lin fanno col canto
Le antifone salire al sommo Donno,
Che nate in Oriente e poi, compito
Del globo il giro, han fin sopra quel lito.

IV.

Ma quando il santo lume illanguidito
Verso il lontano occaso lor declina,
E cominciando va del vespro il lito
Esatto qual la stella vespertina,
Notte in quel punto ha di regnar finito
U' l'uom ne' templi orientai s'inchina:
Nuov' alba a destar vien nuova preghiera
Sorta pur per girar la terra intera.

V.

Fratelli d' Occidente ! Oh ! come anelo
Vorria mio spirto al vostro esser congiunto,
Allo ch' un inno con fervente zelo
S' erge nel tempio dell' offerta al punto;
Pensando quale ei d' spazio di cielo
Varcar pria che sul labbro a voi sia giunto,
Ripetuto via via di gente in gente
Finchè tra voi l'estremo Amen si sente.

VI.

Pria che il fosse da me, quell' inno stesso
Cantato fu nei templi d'Inghilterra,
Ed in barbara lingua forse espresso
Pei colli e i pian che l' Oriente serra:

E per morir nel più cupo recesso
Da pinti muri e vôlte, u' si disserra,
S' innoltra in selve il cui denso fogliame
Copre il selvaggio dal color di rame.

VII.

Lo spirto mio commuovesi all' idea
Che il nostro vincitor rito Anglicano,
Dall' Isola fedele uscir potea
Per unir tanti cor di mano in mano!
Un segno egli è che Dio ne concedea
Contro il crudele anátema romano:
Suggel vital, fuoco divin che suole
Ardere, o Madre, in queste tue parole:

VIII.

Una—nell' acqua consacrata, il dritto
  Sebben per lunga età dimenticato;
Una—nel sangue di Gesù traffitto,
  Benchè l' abbia l' alter Trento negato;
Una—in spirito e senza alcun conflitto
  Con ogni antica parte e dritto usato;
Deh! fa sì, ch' io per sempre, o Madre mia,
Una con CRISTO, una con Te mi sia.

LE CAMPANE A FESTA IN INGHILTERRA.

I.

SQUILLE ah ! squille del loco nativo,
   D 'Inghilterr la verde, l'antica,
   Il cui suon per mill' anni festivo
   Dalle torri ederose s' udì !
Com' è lieta la musica loro
   Quando all' alba d'un giorno solenne
   Pari a voce d'angelico coro,
   A pregar tutto un popolo unì !

II.

Mille storie un tal suono di festa,
   Vecchie storie sì grate ricorda:
   Mille a Prima ed a Vespro ridesta
   Commoventi memorie nel cor.
Nozze e morte al mendico, al sovrano
   Proclamando con voce imparziale,
   Benedetto, solenne, cristiano
   Delle squille rimbomba il fragor.

III.

Questo suon che nel patrio soggiorno
   L' alba annunzia del santo Natale,
   Come fecero gli angioli un giorno
   Sulla cuna del Bimbo divin ;
Come allegro all' intorno si spande
   Pe' tugurj, pegli ampli castelli,
   Con gran pompa di tende e ghirlande
   Per ornare un sì fausto mattin !

IV.

Scendon gai d' Inghilterra i tintinni
Dei torrion dalle gotiche aguglie,
Mentre echeggian d'antifone e d' inni
L' ali supe del tempio maggior;
Ove il sacro splendor, che dei preti
Sovra il capo rifletta, rischiara
Di baudiere le adorne pareti,
I festoni intrecciati di fior.

V.

Quando vien primavera gioconda
Suonan liete di Pasqua le squille,
E il lor suono t'allegra, t' innonda,
D' ere sante, o Regina fedel.
Pari a scolte i lor suoni van pronti
Echeggiando d'altura in altura:
Dalle valli alle cime de' monti
Van gridando: E risorto l' Agnel!

VI.

V' amo, o squille del nostra paese,
  Coll' ardor di quest' anima io v' amo:
  Benedico il Signor, che d'inglese
  Vecchio tronco discender mi fe'.
Qual suo figlio il cantar mi diletta
  Che dell' Anglia le glorie proclama;
  E per voi, sacri bronzi, ella è accetta
  Al cospetto del Rege dei re.

VII.

Rede anch' io di sua storia famosa,
Benchè nato a rimota distanza,
T' amo io pur mia contrada selvosa
Che la gioja del mondo puoi far.
Tua la voce materna rimane,
E qui dove il Signore ha suo regno,
Squille inglesi da torri cristiane
Il deserto faran rimbombar.

CRONACHE.

STORIA D'ALCUNE RUINE.

I.

BADIE, pilastri, arcate
D' antiche cattedrali un dì superbe
Piangon le lor navate
Or ricoperte sol d' edera e d' erbe.
Ahi! le vetuste cadono
Vôlte, e sol gufi e pipistrei là sono,
Ove in ginocchio il popolo
Alzava un giorno del *Te Deum* il suono.

II.

E sacri essi non erano
Al Padre nostro, e l' onor suo non v' era?
Forse il Signor fuggíasi
Dalla santa magion della preghiera?

Essi, al par del ricetto
   U' riposa Giacob, sacri un dì furo ;
Ogni altar come il petto
   Della Vergine Madre erane puro.

III.

Oh ! tristo il dì che l' empio
   Roman ne addusse ed il fatal suo regno,
Spiegando in ogni tempio
   Di sua porpora impura il lusso indegno,
Sinchè de gemme ornaronsi
   La mitra e 'l pastoral con pompa estrema,
E profanati furono
   Col vano orpel di regio dïadema!

IV.

Pure il Padre superno
   Ancor ci amava, e ancora il luogo santo
Sul colle antico eterno
   Spiegò di gloria e di bellezza il vanto.
Calpestar 'ne il retaggio
   Quegli uomini ch' avean di ferro il core ;
Ma schiuso al nostro omaggio
   Sorse di nuovo il tempio del Signore

II.

I MARTIRI RIFORMANO LA CHIESA.

I.

Badie, pilastri, arcate
   Di vecchie cattedrali, antiche vôlte,
Vostre sante navate
   Han de' martiri l'ossa in seno accolte.
L' alto barone e 'l vescovo
   Inginocchiati l'un dell' altro accanto
Qui lacrimando supplici
   I lor voti innalzar' de' santi al Santo.

II.

Il tiranno onde espellere
   Dal bel seno dell' angliche contrade,
Come i lor padri, u' sorsero
   Contro quelle di Roma empie masnade;
Poich' essi i templi amavano
   U' regnò Fede in suo candor natio,
Benchè pur troppo gli uomini
   Osasser là di surrogarsi a Dio.

III.

Badie, pilastri, arcate
   D' ogni antica risorta cattedrale,
Delle vostre navate
   L' incenso ancor su per le vôlte sale:

Ancor s' ergo nell' anglico
   Nobil sermon l'antifona cristiana,
Ed oltre il fiume l'organo
   Fa la cheta echeggiar valle lontana.

IV.

Vescovi, preti e diaconi,
   In puri immacolati paramenti
L' Eucaristia, le Supplici
   Preci là sono ad alternare intenti.
Dalle festive e libere
   Squille i fedeli convocati sono,
Chè trionfò l' Altissimo,
   E sua voce rimbomba entro quel suono.

III.

SOLO I REGICIDI PRODUCONO LA DISSENSIONE.

I.

Badie, pilastri, arcate
   Antiche benedette cattedrali,
Salde al tremuoto siate
   E dell' empie discordie ai dì fatali.
Chè non romani artigli
   Questa umiliar potran vecchia Inghilterra,
Ma del suo grembo i figli
   Sono i nemici ch' or le fanno guerra.

II.

Entro i templi un bagliore
Fiammeggia e sordo un mormorio s' intende:
Non di culto è splendore,
Nè suon di preci che devoto ascende.
Di sangue il braccio intriso
Un re beffeggian che cadea lor preda;
Di glo riail Sir distruggere
Vorrìan per tema ch' Ei qual re non rieda.

III.

Or masnadier sacrilego
I luoghi ove i fedeli orar' curvati
Calca, e 'l cener d'un vescovo
Va calpestando co' tallon ferrati.
Ora i cavalli sdrajansi
U' già s'inginocchiar' martiri santi,
Nitrendo ove le antifone
Un dì s'ergeano e i salmi al cor parlanti.

IV.

Dal finestron già splendido
Di luce un fiume giù pioveva un giorno,
E coi sacri dell' iride
Color gli oggetti irradiava intorno:
Ma i pinti vetri in polvere
Irne, e dei padri profanar' si l'ossa;
La fonte, ove il battesimo
S' ebber, del sangue de' fratelli é rossa.

IV.

E COMPIONO IL SETTANTESIMO QUARTO SALMO.

I.

Badie, pilastri, arcate
 Antiche e care cattedrali, oh! quanto
Trema chi v' ama! e armate
 Orde nemiche van gioendo intanto.
Pur la prece ancor mormora
 Di vostre litanie spargendo il suono:
Ancor fedeli ha l'Anglia
 Che pregan sempre pel suo re, pel trono.

II.

Nelle capanne il nobile,
 Mentre il villano entro il castel dimora,
Si prostra, qual se l' aere
 La vostra squilla percuotesse ancora:
Può l' Anglia a mane, a sera
 Ne' più abbietti mirar tugurj suoi,
Di fidi eletta schiera
 Tuttor benedicente al rege, a voi.

III.

Lor lezïoni i vescovi
 Van recitando ancor fra le ritorte:
Oh! come i buoni soffrono
 Mentre agli empi sorride ingiusta sorte!

Come a Dio cara è un' anima
 Cui spesso danna un folle plebiscito!
Oh! come l' unto Davide
 Precipitato fu dal trono avito!

IV.

Con essi i lor salteri
 Cui gemon su' bei rabeschi e le sculture,
Ne' templi, già alteri,
 A gara devastar' martello e scure:
Sulle ruine gemono
 Che van coprendo la contrada intera,
E del Signor nel tempio
 Sull' ondeggiante del tiran bandiera.

V.

MA DIO È CON NOI SINO ALLA FINE.

I.

Badie, pilastri, arcate
 Oh! come poche e a gran distanza sparse!
Di vostre glorie andate
 Splendidi i resti ancor potean mirarse.
Mille delubri ahi! caddero:
 Nottole e gufi là annidati or sono,
U' genuflesso il poplo
 Un giorno alzava del *Te Deum* il suono.

II.

Ma i sassi lor, la polvere
Son prezïosi agli occhi della Fede.
E già i baroni riedono
Ai lor castelli, e al soglio il re sen riede.
Di nuovo un lieto e libero
Suon di squille echeggiò di balza in balza:
Ed ogni chiesa in giubilo
Il canto del *Te Deum* di nuovo innalza.

III.

Per nostra madre or supplici
Preghiam: che l'Inghilterra a lungo viva,
Sia grande, santa, libera,
E in mezzo alle sue glorie ognor giuliva:
Sia benedetta ogni anima
Che benedice a lei: dentro a' suoi muri
Sia pace; e gioja stabile
Ne' palagi, nell' aule, e nei tuguri.

IV.

Tutti, o preganti in anglica
Lingua, per l'Inghilterra a Dio pregate:
E prima tu, mia patria,
In questa nuova di tua gloria etate.
Pregate che non riedano
Que' dì che fur per lei giorni tremendi;
Per la tua madre, o figlia,
Prega, e 'l Signor propizio all' Anglia rendi!

NOTES.

I.

ST. SACRAMENT.

LAKE GEORGE—the most beautiful sheet of water in the state of New York—was called *Horicon* by the Aborigines; but by the French missionaries was named *St. Sacrément*, because they deemed its waters too pure for any thing but the holy Sacrament of Baptism, and are said to have sent specimens to France, to be used for that purpose. The Royal American army gave the lake its popular name in compliment to the reigning sovereign, and as a token of their attachment to the house of Hanover.

The visit commemorated in the ballad was made in the summer of 1839.

Page 17.—*The Bloody Pond.* A dark-looking, little, circular pond, near the southern extremity of the lake, is so called from its having been the receptacle of the bodies of the English and Americans, who were massacred by the Indians after the capitulation of Fort William Henry, in the old French war.

Page 19.—*Fort George.* The ruins of this fort are yet in preservation; but of Fort William Henry nothing but mounds and embankments remain.

Page 21.—*Katydid.* A beautiful American insect, whose note

is very striking in the autumnal evening music of American landscapes. It is a delicate kind of grasshopper, and its colour is a beautiful pea-green. Its name is derived from its note, which it incessantly repeats—*katy-did, katy-did*—to the great amusement of listening children.

Page 21.—*Sachems.* Some of my readers may not know that such is the aboriginal term for the Indian chiefs.

Page 22.—*Emerald islets.* The surface of the lake is broken by innumerable little islands, some of them but a few feet in diameter, which look as if they merely floated on the water. You are told by the boatmen, who row you about, that the islands are just one for every day in the year: an assertion which I cannot dispute.

Page 23.—*Distant Thung.* This fine mountain, which some spell Tongue mountain, is the limit of one's view to the northward, from the walls of Fort George.

Page 24.—*Its brimming urn.* Lake George may well be called an overflowing basin, for its outlet is a rapid and descending stream, which, after making a succession of beautiful waterfalls, finds its way into Lake Champlain.

Page 25.—*Monroe.* This name, with those of Montcalm and Uncas, is familiar to all readers, from that beautiful romance of Mr. Cooper, The Last of the Mohicans.

Page 32.—*St. Sacrament for aye.* It is not intended here to express any high estimate of the French Missions among these savages. In general, they merely changed the superstitions of the barbarians, without improving their moral or social condition.

II.

DREAMLAND.

Page 41.—*Had flowers and wreaths.* This practice, once of ordinary occurrence in England, is thus explained by that true-hearted Churchman, John Evelyn, in his Sylva: "We adorn their graves with flowers and redolent plants, just emblems of the life of man, which has been compared in Holy Scriptures to those fading beauties, whose roots being buried in dishonour, rise again in glory."

Page 44.—*Angel lullabies.* The consoling text—"I heard a voice from heaven," &c., is sometimes chaunted at the grave, according to the Rubric; and may be said in poetry to *make that slumber good* which is thus hallowed and blessed.

III.

CAROL.

The decoration of churches and churchyards with evergreens and flowers, and such customs as those of "the Rushbearing," and "Posy Sunday," which are still extant in England, though wholly voluntary, and not ordained by the Church, are, with unprejudiced persons, a beautiful illustration of the faculty by which her spirit invests every good gift of GOD with sacred assqciations.

The holy George Herbert speaks as follows in his Country Parson: "The country parson is a lover of old customs, if they be good and harmless, and the rather because country people are much addicted to them; so that to favour them therein is to win their hearts, and to oppose them therein is to deject them. If there be any ill in the custom which may be severed from the good, he pares the apple, and gives them the clean to feed on." Again: "The country parson takes order that the church be swept and kept clean, ... and at great festivals strewed and stuck with boughs, and perfumed with incense."

So Wordsworth, in his Ecclesiastical Sketches, describes a day among the parishes of Westmoreland, where the village children are accustomed to come forth:

———"by rustic music led,
Through the still churchyard, each with garland gay,
That carried, sceptre-like, o'er tops the head
Of the proud bearer."

It is by such spontaneous and instinctive tributes, precisely such in principle as were ordained in the Old Testament, and accepted in the New (Nehemiah viii. 15 ; St. Matthew xxi. 8), that the beautiful gifts of God are severed from vain and worldly uses, and made to minister to a sanctified taste in Christians of full years: while for children they perform a useful part, in making the associations of their religion attractive and lovely.

IV.

ENGLAND.

IN this ballad, such feelings toward the mother-country are expressed, as I am happy to suppose, not personal to myself, but common to nearly all educated and liberal-minded Americans.

Page 64.—*Baliol men.* Perhaps I should rather have apostrophized the Men of Belial, than the respectable society named in the text; but a college that once had such a man as Southey for a member, can afford to bear a little responsibility for his juvenile Jacobinism. The apostrophe was suggested by his mean little poem on "the Chapel Bell," written in 1793. The young *pantisocrat* seems to have had a peculiar spite against that bell, as another of his poems begins with the hemistich, "Toll on, toll on, old bell!"

Page 65.—*Quiet Corpus.* I have an impression that Corpus must be a quiet place for a moderate reading man, not over studious, and fond of conversation. What can be got from books and pictures gives an American this impression; but I know nothing about it, and am very likely wide of the mark.

V.

CHRONICLES.

PAGE 73.—*Altars all as spotless.* This refers to the early British Church in its original independence, purity, and poverty, before the conversion of the Saxons by St. Augustine, A.D. 596.

Page 73.—*Oh, wo! the hour.* Not the hour of Augustine's mission and patriarchate: for he was sent to convert the Saxons by the good and great Gregory, who abhorred the idea of a supremacy; but the hour *when the pall was imposed,* with an oath of subjection, in the days of William Rufus, against every principle of apostolical precedent and canon law.

Page 75.—*To chase away the tyrant.* The English Reformation was no revolution. It merely threw off the usurped supremacy of the Bishop of Rome, and restored the Church to her primitive purity and independence; rejecting whatever was papal, but carefully retaining all that was apostolical.

Page 76.—*A nation shouteth round.* For the first twelve years of Elizabeth, the papists themselves frequented the sacraments and ministry of the ancient Church of England; showing that in nothing had its identity been lost, or its Catholicity impaired, even in their estimation. During that period two popes had offered to receive and approve the Common Prayer, if the Queen would but consent to the papal supremacy—so that, even in their judgment, the Church had forfeited nothing essential to Catholicity, by translating and reforming her worship. Thus, till 1569, when Pius V. forced those Englishmen who were in favour of his supremacy to become recusants, there was in England *one* pure and undivided Church, which, but for the Romish and Puritan schisms which soon followed, would have become the joy of the whole earth, for beauty and primitive completeness. The recusancy of 1569 was the origin of the papal sect in England, which has no thread of connection with the ancient Church of England; and owes its existence, as well as its creed, to the novelties of the pseudo-council of Trent.

Page 79.—*The noble in the cottage.* Sir Walter Scott has beautifully introduced this fact into his fine fiction, the story of Woodstock, where Alice Lee and Dr. Rochecliffe at their devotions are so beautifully portrayed.

Page 80.—*Their Psalter.* See Psalm lxxiv. 5–10, 20–24. Hearing it read, one Sunday during divine service, at St. Mark's in the Bowery, suggested these verses.

Bishops White and Madison, from whom (with Bp. Provoost) all our clergy have descended, were consecrated at Lambeth, Feb. 4, 1787; and landed in the New World on Easter-day succeeding, to begin a succession which already has its representatives at the antipodes.

VI.

SCOTLAND.

In a collection of letters on the Scottish Church, printed in London in 1690, says Mr. Sage, afterward a Scottish bishop, "I can affirm with a well-grounded assurance, that if by the people you mean the Commonalty . . . the *third man*, throughout the whole kingdom, is not Presbyterian; and if by the people you mean those who are persons of quality and education, I dare boldly say not the *thirteenth*." And even, at the present day—if I may trust an article in Blackwood's, attributed to Professor Wilson—the following is a just account of things: "The greater part of the Scotch aristocracy and landed men (the infinitely greater part of them) are not members of the Kirk of Scotland at all. They are, as all their forefathers were, Episcopalians. They yield, as their ancestors did, to the voice of the majority of the gross population." See *Noctes Ambrosianæ*.

Page 91.—*Shall flout them.* For a very graphic description of the poor appearance which the Kirk makes in Glasgow Cathedral, and some fine remarks thereon, see "Peter's Letters," (No. lxvii.) by Lockhart.

And shame the Church, &c. The American Church owes its episcopate to the persecuted and almost extinguished Church of Scotland, which not only gave to America her first bishop, in the person of Seabury, but by so doing was the means of securing the Lambeth consecrations, with which that from Scotland was united. (See Bp. Wilberforce's American Church, page 194.) Thus she may be said to have put her more flourishing sister to shame.

Page 92.—*The fishwife's voice.* The story of Jenny Geddes, and her exploit in the High Church of St. Giles', Edinburgh (July 23, 1637), is probably familiar to my reader, but may be found in Tales of a Grandfather, Second Series.

Page 92.—*Braes of Ross.* The old see of Ross has once more a bishop.

Page 93.—*The Moray Shepherd.* No Scottish bishop is more venerated in America, than the late good bishop of Moray (Dr. Jolly), who should have been buried in Elgin Cathedral, where many of his predecessors lie entombed.

Page 93.—*Glenalmond.* The founding of Trinity College, near Perth, is hailed by the friends of the Church of Scotland, as an earnest of better days at hand.

VII.

SEABURY'S MITRE.

SAMUEL SEABURY, Bishop of Connecticut, and first Bishop of the American Church, was consecrated at Aberdeen, in Scotland, November 14, 1784. He died Feb. 25, 1796.

Page 96.—*Crown of thorn.* The mitre is of black satin adorned with gold-thread needlework. The Cross is embroidered on the front; and on the reverse, a truly significant emblem, the crown of thorns.

Page 95.—*Her old Regalia.* The discovery of the ancient Regalia of Scotland in 1817, was the subject of great national enthusiasm; and the royal jewels are now preserved in the castle of Edinburgh, as symbols of the independence of the kingdom.

VIII.

RUSTIC CHURCHES.

PAGE 100.—*St. Joseph's thorn.* The celebrated Glastonbury thorn, which blooms at Christmas, is fabled to have been the staff of St.

Joseph of Arimathea, when he came into England as a missionary, A.D. 65. In its immediate vicinity stood the earliest British Church, described by old Fuller as follows:—

"It had in length sixty feet and twenty-six in breadth, made of rods, wattled or interwoven. . . . Let not stately modern churches disdain to stoop, with their highest steeples, reverently doing homage to this poor structure as their first platform and precedent. And let their chequered pavements no more disclaim this oratory's plain floor, than its thatched covering doth envy their leaden roofs." Eccles. Hist., vol. i. p. 14. London, 1837.

IX.

CHURCHYARDS.

The parish of St. George's, Hempstead, is the oldest in the state of New York; and its churchyard, though not a model cemetery, is dear to me as containing the remains of my kinsman, Edward Henry Hyde, some time a member of the University of New York, and at the time of his death intended for Holy Orders. This ballad was suggested by a moonlight visit to his grave, in 1840.

X.

TRINITY, OLD CHURCH.

The removal of the old Trinity church was a sad sight to many New Yorkers; notwithstanding the proposed splendours of the new church. I had often worshipped in it in my boyhood; and just as its destruction was beginning, had a final opportunity of paying my vows there on my twenty-first anniversary, Friday, May 10, 1839.

Page 110.—*Effigy.* The statue of Bishop Hobart, now in the sacristy of the new church, filled the place of an altar-piece in the old church.

XI.

TRINITY, NEW CHURCH.

This church was consecrated on Ascension-day, 1846, when I had the satisfaction of being present at the solemnities.

Page 116.—*Mould of doctrine.* The original Greek of Romans vi. 17 (as criticized by a venerated kinsman, in familiar conversation,) suggested this expression, which is a literal translation of what our English version renders—*form of doctrine.*

XII.

ORATORIES.

The custom here commended has had its examples among the best of men of widely differing piety; and I would instance Herbert, Hooker, and Henry Venn. Even in the dullest days of the eighteenth century, it is gratifying to find Dr. Johnson recommending it on one occasion to his friend Boswell. See Life of Johnson, i. 397. Dublin.

Page 125.—*The Psalmist's cedars.* See Psalm xcii. 11, 12.

XIII.

LITTLE WOODMERE.

Had the Church, as it is in the English Prayer-book, been allowed its quiet and natural development during the seventeenth century, it would have been found in every English village as I have portrayed it in this ballad. Such Herbert, and Ferrar, and Hooker would have had it; and, in our own days, Bishop Heber.

Page 128.—*When the Litany, &c.* "It was a custom in several churches to toll a bell while the Litany was reading, to give notice to the people that the Communion Service was coming on." Wheatley.

Page 130.—*On the north.* It was the custom of our ancestors to bury outcasts and criminals on the shady side of the church.

XIV.

DESOLATIONS.

In the diocese of Virginia, such ruins as are here described unhappily abound.

XV.

CHELSEA.

The General Theological Seminary of the American Church is situated in that quarter of New York known as Chelsea.

Page 139.—*When old Canute.* See the story in Sharon Turner's Anglo-Saxons. Canute himself composed a ballad upon the occasion, of which a fragment remains:

> "Merry sang the monks in Ely,
> When Canute the king was sailing by;
> Row, ye knights, near the land,
> And let us hear the monks' song."

Such is Turner's translation. Wordsworth has a beautiful sonnet on this incident.

XVI.

VIGILS.

The Latin lines at the end of every stanza are the titles of anthems or chants appropriate to the hours.

Page 144.—*Adeste Fideles.* Hither ye faithful.

Page 145.—*Veni Creator.* Come Holy Ghost: as in the Ordinal.

Page 145.—*Jubilate Deo.* The hundredth Psalm.

Page 145.—*Cum Angelis.* With Angels, &c.: as in the Eucharist.

Page 145.—*Nisi Dominus.* Unless the Lord keep the city, the watchman waketh but in vain. Psalm cxxvii.

NOTES. 233

Page 146.—*De Profundis.* Psalm cxxx.

Page 146.—*Kyrie Eleison.* Lord have mercy upon us: as in the Litany.

Page 146.—*Miserere.* Psalm lvii.

Page 147.—*Dies Iræ.* The day of wrath.

Page 147.—*Sursum Corda.* Lift up your hearts: as in the Eucharist.

Page 147. *Fili David.* O son of David: as in the Litany.

Page 147.—*Veni Jesu.* Come, Lord JESUS.

Page 148.—*Nunc Dimittis.* Now, Lord, lettest Thou Thy servant depart in peace. The song of Simeon, St. Luke ii. 29.

XVII.

THE CURFEW.

THE anecdote of William I., which is employed in this ballad, will be found in nearly all English histories. The Curfew-bell, an institution of that monarch, is generally understood.

Page 152.—*New England village.* So late as the beginning of the present century, the nine-o'clock-bell is said to have been generally obeyed in New England, as the warning to go to bed.

XVIII.

NASHOTAH.

AT Nashotah, in Wisconsin, a thousand miles from the Atlantic coast, is a religious establishment of unmarried missionaries, who live and labour in the spirit of the primitive day. All that is said of it and them in this ballad is literally true.

The founders of this mission (and among them was the dear friend to whom this book is dedicated) were, in 1840, my fellow-students at Chelsea, and Wisconsin was then a wilderness. It is now (1850) a Christian diocese, and has a bishop, and twenty-one clergy,—the blessed results, in a great degree, of the self-denying labours of the brethren of Nashotah.

Page 162.—*The Norway rover.* Wisconsin is rapidly filling up with the better class of emigrants from Europe; and the itinerant brothers of Nashotah have under their care settlements of Norwegians, Swedes, Irish, Welsh, English, and Oneida Indians. They have also baptized several Jews.

Page 162.—*The sad Oneida.* Several Oneida Indians are training for Holy Orders at Nashotah; and at the first Diocesan council of Wisconsin, in 1847, there were present several Oneidas, lay delegates. They had walked two hundred miles to be present, and on the last day had accomplished forty-five miles. One of them spoke in debate: probably for the first time (says my friend, the Rev. Dr. Kip) that an American Indian has been heard in the councils of the Church.

XIX.

ST. SILVAN'S BELL.

When this ballad was written, it was a mere a fiction. The Nashotah missionaries have since erected a church, by the name of St. Silvanus, and it can hardly be doubted that the effects anticipated in the ballad have resulted in some degree.

XX.

THE CHURCH'S DAUGHTER.

Page 165.—*Rose-marine.* I have taken a quaint sort of license with the botanical name of the flower rosemary (*rosmarinus*), which has no reference to the rose at all, but is similar in sound. I judge it not out of place in a ballad. The custom of using rosemary at funerals is thus explained by Wheatley, on the Common Prayer:

"To express their hopes that their friend is not lost forever, each person in the company usually bears in his hand a sprig of rosemary: a custom which seems to have taken its rise from a practice among the heathens, of a quite different import. For they have no thought of a future resurrection, but believing that the bodies of those that were dead would forever lie in the grave, made use of cypress at their funeral, which is a tree that being once cut never revives, but dies way. But Christians, on the other side, having better hopes, and knowing that this very body of their friend, which they are now going solemnly to commit to the grave, shall one day rise again, and be reunited to his soul, instead of cypress distribute rosemary to the company, which being always green, and flourishing the more for being cropt (and of which a sprig only being set in the ground, will sprout up immediately and branch into. a tree), is more proper to express their confidence and trust."

THE END.

www.ingramcontent.com/pod-product-compliance
Lightning Source LLC
Chambersburg PA
CBHW032140230426
43672CB00011B/2397